THE OFFICIAL RULE BOOK FOR THE
New
CHURCH GAME

KEN HEMPHILL

BROADMAN PRESS
NASHVILLE, TENNESSEE

The Official Rule Book for the New Church Game

ISBN: 0-8054-6011-X
Dewey Decimal Classification: 262.7
Subject Heading: CHURCH
Library of Congress Catalog Card Number: 89-37254

Printed in the United States of America

Library of Congress Cataloging-in-Publication Data

Hemphill, Kenneth S., 1948-
    The official rule book for the new church game / Ken Hemphill.
        p.   cm.
    ISBN 0-8054-6011-X
    1. Church.   I. Title.
BV600.2.H394   1990
262—dc20
                                                                89-37254
                                                                CIP

Inside illustrations by Tad Crisp

To the members of First Baptist, Norfolk,
who have modeled these biblical
principles in the laboratory of life.

Preface

The Burning Conviction

All those who had believed were together, and had all things in common; and they began selling their property and possessions, and were sharing them with all, as anyone might have need. And day by day continuing with one mind in the temple, and breaking bread from house to house, they were taking their meals together with gladness and sincerity of heart, praising God, and having favor with all the people. And the Lord was adding to their number day by day those who were being saved (Acts 2:44-47).

Can we dare to believe that we could belong to a Christian community like the one described in this passage in Acts? Was that church simply a New Testament phenomenon? Can we expect a dimension of fellowship that expresses itself in a joyful, spontaneous, practical fashion? Is it possible to find a church family where the people are of one mind? Should we dream of a growing church so effective that those who are being saved are being added to our number day by day?

These have become burning issues in both my own personal Bible study and in my ministry. My heart's desire is to be involved in a dynamic, growing, and ministering community. I have found that this is the desire of pastors and lay people everywhere. If we could only become what God has called us to be! My heart's burning conviction is that God has not changed, nor has His desire, commission, or empowering of the church been altered. I believe that the 1990s could be the decade of revival and unprecedented church growth.

The Troubling Facts

The church of the last three decades in America has been largely ineffective. Numerous church growth experts have pointed to the downward trend in virtually every major denomination beginning in the early 1960s. Certainly there have been exceptions. My own denomination, the Southern Baptists, have inched ahead over the past thirty years, but there is troubling evidence that we have lost the vision of explosive expansion that propelled us in the 1940s and 1950s. Smaller and newer denominational groups in America have chalked up impressive gains in the last two decades, but when weighed against the losses suffered by many of the major denominations, we would still find insignificant gains in the larger body of believers.

A recent speech by George Gallup, the famous pollster, pointed to other disturbing facts about the state of religion worldwide. Belief in a personal God who answers prayers and judges persons—the God of biblical revelation—declined between 1974 and 1981. For example, less than one-fourth of the people in Western Europe believe that the Ten Commandments still apply to "most people." Gallup found that many people interviewed claimed to revere the Bible as the inspired Word of God, but in turn revealed a shocking ignorance of basic biblical facts. Fewer than half of all adults can name the four Gospels of the New Testament. Only four in ten college graduates know that Jesus delivered the Sermon on the Mount. Gallup fears that the cycle of biblical illiteracy is likely to continue since today's teenagers know even less about the Bible than do adults.

Beyond the knowledge of biblical facts, Christians surveyed admitted that they did not have a good grasp of the "how-to" aspects of living the Christian life. Many Christians do not see any connection between their religious commitment and social issues. Their commitment to Christ and His church is a surface-only commitment. Gallup concluded: "America on the surface is a remarkably religious nation, but other facts suggest that our nation should be a prime target for evangelistic efforts."

Encouraging Signs

Gallup's report, however, contained several encouraging signs. The cumulative evidence shows a slowing of the downtrends in religious belief. In other words, we may have found the bottom in religious apathy and may be poised for another era of church growth and evangelistic outreach. The latest figures concluded that 79 percent of the world's people are religious compared to 72 percent in 1970, with the proportion of outright disbelievers declining from 13 percent to 4.4 percent. Americans ranked at the top in the rating of the importance of God in their lives. Ninety percent of Americans believe in a personal God or some sort of spirit or life force. A whopping 84 percent believe in a Heavenly Father who watches over us and can be reached by our prayers. Perhaps most exciting is the fact that 40 percent of Americans attend church or synagogue every week. A huge 81 percent of Americans consider themselves Christians.

What a tremendous opportunity we have in the church today! If 40 percent of our population attend church or synagogue weekly and the level of spiritual hunger is growing, a dynamic New Testament church has unparalleled opportunities to reach its community for Christ. If we can but demonstrate the life-changing power of the gospel, teach people the Bible, and encourage them in practical Christian living, we can penetrate our nation and change the world.

Indeed, we are seeing signs of spiritual awakening. In every community there are a few churches who are experiencing explosive growth. Multiple worship services and Sunday Schools are becoming the way of life for many church families. Yet down the street and in the very shadow of these growing churches are churches on the decline. Can churches everywhere experience the supernatural empowering of Holy God? Can we restore the vitality that made the early New Testament community in Jerusalem so appealing? Can your church grow? I believe so. I am bullish on the church. The best days are still in our future. We must begin with a renewed look at the biblical foundations of the church.

The Purpose of This Study

My initiative in writing this book comes out of my love for the church and my conviction that the church is the body of Christ, the very cutting edge of spiritual awakening and world evangelization. We must recognize our potential, commit ourselves to the task, and experience the full empowering of God's Spirit. The church triumphant can and must become reality. We must become what we have been called to be. We cannot approach our involvement in the local church with a casual attitude that is inappropriate to our high calling. This is not a game! We're not dealing with issues as simple as life and death —but we are dealing with eternal issues. Our very best is required.

This book was born from a series of sermons preached initially at First Baptist Norfolk, a church family who has taught me many invaluable lessons about being the church. Much of the sermonic flavor will still be evident. The illustrations have occasionally been altered to protect the innocent. In other instances, the details of the illustrations have been changed by the process of senility and frequent retelling with embellishment. Such embellishment is most often readily apparent. I have sought permission for the use of all illustrations that could be considered personal in nature. I am therefore greatly indebted to those folks who have willingly allowed their stories to be told.

I have made no attempt to cover every aspect of the church's life. There certainly could be greater emphasis on social ministries, missions, worship, and many other facets of the church's work. Numerous books are available that will give the interested reader plenty of help in these areas. This book is very simply a call to be the church and not play church. It is a call to recognize the priority of the church's work.

I am grateful to John and Dot Kautz, members of First Baptist, who helped in the area of proofreading during the early stages of manuscript production. I am indebted to Dr. Kurt Richardson who gave invaluable time to ensure that I didn't make too many foolish theological blunders or overstatements. I am especially appreciative to Diane Styron who laboriously translated this manuscript from handwritten hieroglyphics to a neatly typed version. My entire ministerial staff contributed to this project in ways too numerous to mention. I have already indicated my great indebtedness to the members of First Baptist. Of course, my own family was gracious to give me the time and encouragement to produce this book.

Finally, I am grateful that you have made the commitment to read this book. I trust God will use it mightly in your life and in the life of your church family.

Contents

1

I Never Met the Parker Brothers

Now when Jesus came into the district of Caesarea Philippi, He began asking His disciples, saying, "Who do people say that the Son of Man is?" And they said, "Some say John the Baptist; and others, Elijah; but still others, Jeremiah, or one of the prophets." He *said to them, "But who do you say that I am?" And Simon Peter answered and said, "Thou art the Christ, the Son of the living God." And Jesus answered and said to him, "Blessed are you, Simon Barjona, because flesh and blood did not reveal this to you, but My Father who is in heaven.

—Matthew 16:13-17

When it comes to games, no one enjoys playing more than I. Perhaps my enthusiasm for games came from my early childhood. Some of my earliest memories are of our family game nights. We played Old Maid, Authors, and Parchessi. Being the youngest child, I rarely won, but I still loved to play.

Often during the Christmas season, we shopped for a new family game. My eyes were wide with amazement as I saw the number of games that could be purchased. I noticed that many of these games were by the Parker Brothers. Who were these guys? Were they really brothers? Where did they come up with all the neat ideas? I still don't know the answers to all those questions, but I still enjoy the games they created. It wasn't important to meet the Parker Brothers in order to play their games. All I had to do was read the instructions, get the game board out, and enjoy the game.

Since the early 1960s most major denominations in the Unit-

ed States have experienced either a decline or they have pla-
teaued. At the same time there is widespread evidence that
there is a growing hunger for spiritual matters. Could it be that
we have been guilty of going about our church activities and
programs as if they were a "new church game?" We shop for
a new program, unpackage it, read the directions, and start to
play. Everyone becomes involved in the game, but we see few
results.

For example, in my first full-time pastorate I wanted desperately to make a good impression. I had an idea that would
humanize my ministry and at the same time give our church
a more intimate and personal feeling. I determined that I
would position myself each Sunday morning in our covered
drive-through, open the car door for the ladies, and personally
welcome each family as they arrived for Sunday School. I had
been the pastor of First Church for only a few weeks when I
began this new project. It met with mixed results. Some were
delighted and impressed with the service and the servant attitude of the new pastor. Some were a bit annoyed as they were
making last minute adjustments to makeup or just winding up
a family "discussion" about "why we're always late for
church."

One particular lovely Sunday morning as I was fulfilling this
unique pastoral duty, I became fascinated by the rather ani-
mated discussion going on between a young man and his father. They were about three cars back from the drop-off point,
so I was able to observe the conversation for a few moments.
It wasn't too difficult to guess the nature of the disagreement.
The young lad was dressed in his Sunday best. He was obviously unhappy with his buttoned-up collar and clip-on necktie. His
father, on the other hand, looked most comfortable in an open-
collared knit shirt. It was apparent the young man was being
delivered to church while his dad was off to the golf course.
From the gestures and facial expressions I gathered that the
son was pleading his case to accompany his dad to the golf
course, but was losing. As I reached to open the door, the boy
made one last valiant attempt to establish his position: "Dad,
are you sure you went to church when you were a little boy?"

"Yes, Son, I've told you over and over I went every Sunday."

"Well," he retorted, "I bet it won't do me any good either!"

We laugh at that story, but it's a painful, nervous laugh. How could this gentleman go to church for years and there not be any evidence to convince his son of its value? Had he only played a game that produced no results? Or better yet, if it was of value, why had he now found golf to be a greater priority? Perhaps we ought to ask a more fundamental question: Do we *really* believe that what we do at church is of eternal significance? Or are we just playing church?

The church is *no game!* For that reason, we need to take a fresh new look at the doctrine of the church. In my opinion, the New Testament church is the most exciting topic that can be discussed. No organization on the face of this earth has the church's authority, power, or potential. Yet we must reluctantly confess that there is no organization where membership is valued so little. For many folks it is given considerably less priority than their involvement in a community organization or sports club. We will reverse this trend only when we come to a full biblical understanding of the true nature of the church as God intends it to be. We must then start at the place of origin.

The Demanding Question

We need to keep the context of Matthew 16 clearly in focus. The question, "Who do you say I am?" and Peter's answer form the climax to a long section of material that actually began with the inauguration of Jesus' public ministry recorded in Matthew 4:17. At this point Jesus had not yet publicly declared His messianic identity and authority. Nonetheless, it had been clear and unmistakable in both His teaching and His public actions.

This is especially the case in Matthew 12:22-37 where Jesus healed a demon-possessed man. The crowd had speculated concerning whether Jesus could be the "Son of David," a messianic title. The Pharisees had accused Him of casting out demons by the power of Beelzebul. Jesus responded, "But if I cast out demons by the Spirit of God, then the kingdom of God has come upon you." The Jewish leaders clearly understood the messianic overtones of His words and demanded a sign of authentication (12:38). At the beginning of this sixteenth chapter we encounter the Pharisees and Sadducees again demanding from Jesus a sign to authenticate His messianic authority. Jesus responded that they had been able to predict the weath-

er by reading the signs of the sky. The obvious implication is
that they had witnessed plenty of evidence in the works and
words of Jesus, if they would but open their eyes and ears to
the clear signs of Jesus' ministry. Thus Jesus refused to give any
other sign but that of Jonah.

The setting for this conversation is Caesarea Philippi, a non-
Jewish area near the headwaters of the Jordan. It appears to be
a private conversation involving only Jesus and His disciples.
No doubt, as was His custom, Jesus had taken His disciples
aside to give them further instruction.

Jesus first asked, "Who do people say that the Son of Man is?"
(Matt. 16:13) What is the popular opinion?[1] There was a growing consensus that Jesus was one of the prophets. The suggestion that He was John the Baptist may well reflect the opinion
of Herod the tetrarch (14:1-2). It appears that Herod had developed an almost paranoid fear about this prophet who had
challenged his life-style. Those who believed Jesus to be Elijah
saw Him as a forerunner of the messiah, still to be revealed
(Mal. 4:5-6). The identification with Jeremiah perhaps had
emerged because people saw in Jesus' ministry and teaching
a mixture of suffering and authority like that embodied by
Jeremiah. Further, it is likely that they sensed a common chord
in their teaching of impending judgment on Israel.

The critical question now was posed to the disciples, "Who
do you say that I am?" We should never overlook the fact that
this question is as relevant today as it was 2,000 years ago. It
is also a question that every individual must personally face.
The question is not what do others think about Jesus. It is not
so much what your parents or your neighbors or the skeptics
think, but who do you say Jesus is? Have you honestly and
openly confronted and answered that question?

The word translated "you" is emphatic and plural. It is addressed to the disciples as a group. They had been with Jesus.
They had not only seen His public actions and heard His teachings, but also they had enjoyed the benefit of His personal
tutoring. Their understanding should be advanced beyond
that of the general public or even that of the Jewish leaders.

The Daring Confession (vv. 16-17)

I have often tried to recreate this scene in my own imagination. Perhaps the disciples were sitting about an open fire

having just shared an evening meal. After the nonthreatening question concerning the opinion of others, Jesus looked from face-to-face as He posed the demanding question, "Who do you say that I am?" You can almost feel the excitement, the quickening of the pulse rates, the constriction of the throats, and the heavy swallowing as they wondered: *Do we dare say it?* It must have been that these words of confession had nearly burst from their lips on several previous occasions, but they had been choked back. Now their growing conviction could be concealed no longer. Peter, the disciple who often served as a spokesman for the twelve,[2] gave expression to the conviction and hope that had been growing stronger in all of them. His words of confession are direct, simple, and to the point, "Thou art the Christ" (v. 16). *Christ* is the Greek equivalent for the Hebrew *messiah.*

What a daring confession! Can you sense the excitement? The long-awaited Messiah! The King from the line of David! The One whom God had sent to restore His people! The fulfillment of God's promises! The One who would usher in the kingdom of God! The One who was the author of redemption and forgiveness! This was the first occasion in Matthew's Gospel where the messianic title had been used in reported speech.[3] Can you hear the trembling words that must have forced their way out of Peter's lips? You are the Messiah!

We have read or repeated this confession so often that it sometimes fails to create in us the true excitement and wonder that it should. We are so removed from that moment we forget how truly daring it was. In a few short years men and women would die for repeating these words of confession. We must sense again this excitement. Jesus, whom we claim to serve, is God's Messiah: the one and only answer for the sin of the world.

Peter continued his confession: "The Son of the living God." While this event is recorded by both Mark and Luke, Matthew alone included this final element of Peter's confession.[4] It seems likely that Matthew wanted us to understand that Peter's declaration went beyond the nationalistic fervor of Jewish messianic expectation and indicated an awareness of Jesus' special relationship with God.[5] Jesus was not simply a Jewish hero or deliverer but uniquely "the Son of the living God."

It is significant that Peter's confession came in the calm of private inquiry rather than in response to the casting out of demons or the stilling of a storm. Sometimes, in the midst of emotionally charged circumstances, people make confessions concerning that on which they do not follow through. Already in Matthew, some of the crowd had yelled out messianic titles such as "Son of David" in response to Jesus' ministry (9:27; 12:23). For them, confession was still emotional speculation. But Peter's confession marks a crucial stage in the disciples' understanding of Jesus. They had followed Him out of the hope and conviction that He was Messiah. The full understanding of even this confession still awaited the postresurrection experience. We see this in Peter's response to Jesus' announcement that as Messiah He must suffer and die. Nonetheless, this is a significant milestone of growing understanding, conviction, and faith.

Jesus Himself recognized it as such with His response, "Blessed are you, Simon Barjona." Further He declared that this confession was the result of divine revelation, not human reasoning. This declaration was not a response to "signs and wonders" as demanded and yet ignored by the leaders of the Jews, but it was a matter of revelation. Today there appears to be a subtle, or not so subtle, eagerness of some church leaders to highlight "signs and wonders" in evangelism. A close study of New Testament evidence will indicate that "signs and wonders" were not always convincing evangelistic tools in Jesus' day, nor do I think they will prove to be so in our culture today. Ultimately, true saving confession of Jesus as one's personal Savior is by revelation of the Father. Salvation is the internal working of God's Spirit who reveals to us the truth about our sin and His Son.

The Implication of the Confession

It should not be overlooked that the declaration of God's plan to grow a messianic community is bound to the confession of Jesus' messianic identity.[6] The connection is clear in verse 18 where Jesus' reply to Peter is continued, "I also say to you that you are Peter, and upon this rock I will build My church." Here, for the first time, Jesus declared God's eternal plan to build a messianic community made up of those who have a relationship with Him through His Son.

We should note that our view of Christ as the unique Son of

God, the only begotten of the Father, is bound up with our view of the church. If we do not properly and biblically conclude that Jesus is the unique Son of God, the Messiah, God's one answer for the world's sin problem, we have no basis for understanding the unique origin, function, and authority of the New Testament church. If we do not hold to the uniqueness of Jesus, the church becomes nothing more than another institution, at best a divine country club. The other side of the coin is equally true. When we profess to believe that Jesus is the Christ, we cannot treat His church with apathy.

One other passage where this great truth comes to light is in Colossians 1. In the Colossian letter Paul was dealing with heretical teaching that threatened the existence of the church. We can determine from Paul's response that one facet of the heretical teaching was the denial of the uniqueness of Jesus as the Messiah and Savior. This in turn led to a devaluation of the church that was based upon Christ. When Christ was devalued, then the church became nothing more than one of the many mystery religions of that day. Paul began with a prayer that they might be filled with knowledge so that they could walk in a worthy manner (v. 9-10). In verse 12 we find the beginning of one of the greatest Christological statements in all of Scripture as Paul detailed the uniqueness of Christ. Let's look together at these unique claims.

1. *He is the only source of redemption* (1:12-14). In ourselves, we are not fit to share in the heritage of God's people, but in Christ we are qualified. The evidence that we share in the inheritance of the saints is that He has delivered us from the domain of darkness. From the kingdom of darkness we have been transferred to the kingdom of His Son, in whom we have redemption and the forgiveness of sin.

2. *He is the "image of the invisible God"* (v. 15). We must put no limitations on this verse. Paul was declaring that Christ was and is and ever will be the image of God. Christ is the image of God in the sense that He perfectly reveals God. He renders the invisible, visible. Thus this phrase speaks of Jesus' preincarnate glory, His incarnation, and His ultimate glorification, all of which reveal God. Paul was countering a growing theological heresy that identified Christ as a shadowy abstraction revealing God. In our day there are those who claim to believe in Christ, but they put Him on a level with other

prophets and religious leaders who reveal God. The powerful influence of the "New Age" movement seeks to devalue Christ to the level of other religious leaders who reveal God. This text will not allow for such an abstraction.

3. *He is Lord of creation.* He is both the means of God's creative activity and the Sustainer of the universe. The "first-born of all creation" denotes both priority in time and supremacy in authority. Simply put, He was before all creation in time, and He has authority over all creation by virtue of His role in the creation. This phrase does not suggest that He was a part of the created order. Three prepositions define the lordship of Christ in regard to creation. All things were created "by Him," "for Him," and it holds together "in Him." The stacking of phrases in verse 16 was intended to impress upon the reader that as a part of His lordship over creation, He is supreme over all supernatural powers. In our day there is an eagerness to contact the spirit powers within several movements. Why this interest in inferior and dangerous spiritual powers when Christ is supreme over all spiritual beings?

4. *He is head of the church* (v. 18). Sometimes we are awed as we think of the mystery of the universe. We look at the stars, and we read of solar systems and galaxies light years away. It boggles our finite minds. Then we think of the God who created and sustains it. Yet in spite of all the mystery and majesty of God's creation, the climax of this great hymn is found in the affirmation of Christ's supremacy over the church. He is "head" in the sense of being sovereign of the church. There may well be a parallel idea that He is Creator and Sustainer of the church, but the emphasis is on His rule. He alone is sovereign over the church. The word for church is *ekklēsia* or "congregation." It is made up of all the redeemed people of God, and it is the means whereby Christ carries out His mission here on earth. This is the same word Jesus used in Matthew 16:18 when He declared His intention of building a new community.

The paragraph from verses 18-23 explains the basis for Christ's supremacy. He is "first-born" from the dead, the One in whom the "fulness" of God dwells. He alone can reconcile alienated men and women to God. But the focusing of our attention once again should be this unique interlinking of the lordship of Christ and the creation of the church. *His* uniqueness is the basis of *our* uniqueness. We are His new creation—

the zenith of His messianic work. We are a part of God's eternal plan of redemption!

Relevant Questions

This is indeed an awesome truth once it is comprehended. If we look at Colossians 1:25, we hear the wonder in Paul's testimony: "Of *this church* I was made a minister according to the stewardship from God bestowed on me for your benefit." If we do not believe these unique truths about God's Son, we will never fully comprehend the true significance of the church. In turn, our involvement in the church becomes an issue of habit or even convenience that often fades to apathy. For those who deny these unique truths, the church is nothing more than another religious institution.

We also must be challenged by the opposite side of this truth. If we confess to believe these truths, and then we treat the church with apathy or even disdain, it is the worst form of hypocrisy. Our apathy creates a hindrance to evangelism and drains the church of its effectiveness. Our bulging church rolls and declining attendance figures must stand as an indictment against us.

One Sunday evening I was sharing with our new members' class the various statistics of church growth. I was explaining how Sunday School enrollment affects Sunday School attendance. I noted that only about 40 percent to 50 percent of those enrolled will be in attendance on a given Sunday. One bright college student caught the significance of those numbers. "Where are they?" he wondered. "What are we going to do about it?" he questioned. These are penetrating and relevant questions. Are we going to be satisfied with these statistics simply because this is the way it is in all denominations, or can we experience a true revival of commitment?

We must think through other relevant matters. I occasionally hear of so-called Christians who are not involved in a local church. They want to claim membership in the "universal church," but they just can't find a church good enough for them, or they haven't time for a church now. I think we must challenge this unbiblical assumption that a person can belong to some universal church and not confess it through a real-life commitment to a local expression of the church.

We must further question the casual attitude that has

emerged about church attendance, participation, and service. The church is not simply a convenient place to gather, a good place to meet and make friends. It is not simply an organization designed to provide for child care while we play golf or to help us keep our youth in tow. It is not simply an asset to our neighborhood that helps realtors sell homes. The church is Christ's creation, His body, His bride. He died to redeem the church, and He will return for it. Therefore, can we treat it with casual indifference? Too much is at stake not to challenge the apparent apathy of many church members.

I trust that we can address these issues, find biblical answers, and experience revival. Let's unleash the mightiest power ever seen: the church as God planned for it to be! Church is *no game!*

Since church is not a game, we must point to one other difference between our childhood experience of game playing and our church activities. Monopoly can be played without knowing the Parker Brothers, but we can't belong to the church unless we know its Author. Until the disciples confessed that Jesus Christ was their Messiah, God's only Son, they could not understand nor participate in the mission of the church. Until you know Jesus Christ as your personal Savior, you can't be a part of the church, understand its significance, nor experience its divine empowering. It doesn't matter whether you were raised a Baptist, Methodist, Catholic, or whatever; you must still accept Jesus as your personal Savior. You must confess Him as *your* Lord.

Right now you can confess Jesus as Lord if you never have. Here are the important biblical steps to trusting Jesus as your personal Savior: (1) recognize His love for you, (2) admit your need for Him, (3) agree with God about your sin, and (4) invite Jesus to come into your life. You might want to express this in a prayer. Prayer is simply talking to God. "Dear Father, I know you love me. I know that I am a sinner and that I need forgiveness. Right now I invite you into my life. Thank you for saving me." Jesus is your personal Savior. Welcome to the family of God. Tell a pastor or another Christian about your decision.

Notes

1. The title "Son of Man" is omitted in Mark and Luke. It appears to have been a favorite self-designation of Jesus. Obviously, it did not yet contain unambiguous messianic meaning, or Jesus' question here is rather senseless.

2. Matthew presented Peter in the role of a spokesman for the twelve on numerous occasions (14:28; 15:15-16; 17:24-27; 18:21; 19:27; and 26:40).

3. It has been used in Matthew's editorial words in 1:1,16,17,18;2:4; and 11:2, but not in a spoken confession of this nature.

4. Some scholars have attempted to argue that "Son of the living God" is an addition by Matthew. However, Ben F. Meyer has presented a convincing argument for accepting Matthew's form as authentic. See Ben F. Meyer, *The Aims of Jesus* (London:SCM, 1979), 189-191.

5. R. T. France, *Matthew*, vol. 1 *Tyndale New Testament Commentaries* (Grand Rapids: Wm. B. Eerdmans, 1985).

6. Some scholars argue against the authenticity of Matthew 16:18-19, verses which are missing in Mark and Luke. However, no manuscript evidence exists to suggest they were a later addition. I can find no convincing argument for not accepting them as original. For a defense of their originality, see George Eldon Ladd, *The Presence of the Future: The Eschatology of Biblical Realism* (Grand Rapids: Wm. B. Eerdmans, 1974), chapter 10.

2

Red Rover, Red Rover

"And I also say to you that you are Peter, and upon this rock I will build My church; and the gates of Hades shall not overpower it. "I will give you the keys of the kingdom of heaven; and whatever you shall bind on earth shall be bound in heaven, and whatever you shall loose on earth shall be loosed in heaven." Then He warned the disciples that they should tell no one that He was the Christ.

—Matthew 16:18-20

"Red Rover, Red Rover, send Jenny right over!" Jenny, giggling, backed up to get a running start. She clinched her teeth and launched herself forward toward eight, brightly clad children who had joined hands with white-knuckled intensity. Jenny's goal was to try to break through the clasped hands and win the right to carry one of those who had formed that opposing line back to her side. Those extending their clasped arms waited to absorb her blow and enfold her, thus capturing her for their team. The game concluded when all the children had been held and formed one large team.

After Peter's confession that Jesus was the Christ, Jesus revealed His plan for building His church. To this church He promised the keys of the kingdom! These keys, like the clenched hands of the children, have the power to loose or to bind for eternity. What does this suggest concerning the church built upon the confession "Jesus is Lord?"

A Contradictory Survey

A fascinating religious survey appeared in our local newspaper not long ago. I'm not sure how reliable these surveys are, but, occasionally, they do provide interesting statistics that confirm what we are actually seeing in the religious community. The two most fascinating statistics related to belief in Jesus as divine and the relevance of the church. On one hand, the belief that Jesus is divine is growing among those surveyed and stands at an all-time high of 84 percent. However, of those surveyed, only 44 percent believe that the church has any relevance today. This figure, the survey tells us, is at an all-time low.

First, this disparity must serve as clear warning that those of us who are committed to Christ and His church have much work to do. Obviously, our first priority must be that of spiritual renewal. We need a fresh new moving of God's Spirit and power to energize us. Second, we must seek ways to bring timeless truths to bear in our community in a way that is meaningful and relevant to twentieth-century audiences. We must demonstrate and teach that the church is the body of Christ, and thus it is alive and well.

There is one other issue of concern that these statistics raise. No doubt a significant number of the 56 percent of respondents who found the church irrelevant were once active in a church. Why do we have so many members on our rolls who are inactive? Many of them, I suppose, would claim to be born-again believers, yet they sense no need to be involved in the life of a local church. I think these statistics point out the profound need to understand the doctrine of the church. They confront us with the tragic results of ignorance about the nature of the church. There is no other way we can explain the seeming contradiction of the two statistics mentioned above. If we confess Jesus to be divine—the only begotten Son of the Father—how can we at the same moment treat the church as an irrelevant appendage? I'm quite confident that many of the respondents who said they believed Jesus is divine did not mean it in the sense of a wholehearted commitment to Him as their personal Savior. Nevertheless, we are still guilty for not making it crystal clear to our people and the listening world that the confession of Jesus as the Christ and love for His church must go hand in hand.

Our own internally generated statistics must trouble us on this matter. Over half the people on the rolls of our churches are no longer active. Of those that we consider to be active, we fully anticipate that nearly half of them will be absent on a given Sunday. Finally, the most disturbing statistic is that only 20 percent of those who attend regularly contribute in terms of money and time. Must we simply accept these grim statistics? Is there not something we can do? We cannot afford to do nothing! Too much is at stake. A sure point of beginning must be a clear understanding of God's plan for the church.

In the last chapter, we looked briefly at Peter's confession, "Thou art the Christ," as the context for understanding the nature of the church. Only at this point of revelational knowledge did Jesus take a further step to reveal to His disciples the plan and purpose for establishing a new community. Let's go to our text in Matthew 16:18-20 to look at God's plan.

Foundation: "Upon This Rock" (v. 18)

Jesus responded to Peter in the same fashion that Peter had confessed Him: "I also say to you that you are Peter, and upon this rock I will build My church." Peter, as spokesman of the disciples had just declared his belief in the uniqueness of Jesus as God's Messiah, the Redeemer of the world. Thus Jesus similarly declared Peter's (and, consequently, the apostles') unique role in the working out of God's purpose of redemption through the church.

There is a play on words that is obvious in the Greek but not so clear in the English translations. In the statement "you are Peter," the Greek word is *Petros,* which can be translated "stone" or "rock." *Petros* transliterates the underlying Aramaic *Cephas.* This name had been given to Simon at an earlier stage by Jesus. In John 1:42 we read: "He brought him to Jesus. Jesus looked at him, and said, 'You are Simon the son of John; you shall be called Cephas' (which translated means Peter)" (see Mark 3:16). The imagery of a rock was not a reference to the character of Peter but rather to his function as a foundation stone in the building of the church.[1]

Thus Jesus continued, "And upon this rock [*petra*] I will build My church." The most natural reading of this verse based on the word play, the structure of the passage, and content of ✓ the passage is to accept this as a declaration concerning Peter's foundational role in the church.

I must pause here to say that this has not been a position accepted by all evangelical theologians because of Roman Catholic claims that what was said here of Peter applies to later bishops at Rome. This text gives no support for a papal institution. Nothing is said about Peter's successors, infallibility, or exclusive authority.[2] Nonetheless, we should not overreact to this Roman Catholic interpretation and miss the obvious point of this text.

Some scholars in reaction to Catholic teaching have pointed to the change from *petros* to *petra* in the Greek text. They contend that *petros* refers to Peter as a little rock and that *petra* means "stone" or "boulder" and refers to Jesus, the foundation Rock. However, the Greek word for rock (*petra*) would necessarily be changed to the masculine form *petros* for a man's name. More significantly the underlying Aramaic, spoken by Jesus, would have been *kepha,* and the words would have been identical in both places. Furthermore, the suggestion that Jesus is the foundation misses the point of the confession of Peter, and it confuses the imagery of this passage where Jesus is portrayed as the builder.[3]

Other scholars follow another line of debate and suggest that the rock of foundation is not Peter but his confession of faith. This suggestion has more to recommend it, but it misses the whole point of the word play and Jesus' declaration concerning Peter. This thinking, however, is not totally out of line because it is on the basis of Peter's confession that Jesus declared Peter's role as foundational to the building of the church.

Peter, as spokesman of the disciples, is in a sense the "first among equals," and it is on the foundation of the apostles that Jesus planned to build His church. This was not an honor earned nor deserved but a privilege and responsibility that came by way of revelation. Thus, it is Peter—the leader and spokesman of the apostles, the one who first made this apostolic confession—who was a rock on whom Jesus would build His new community. We can conclude by implication that the other disciples, for whom Peter was spokesman, were also foundational to the community. The point of Jesus' declaration was His intention of building a community on the foundation of the apostles and, consequently, their apostolic witness to Him. Thus it is a biblical foundation; it is the witness of divine revelation itself.

It is of course true that in certain contexts such as 1 Corinthians 3:11, "For no man can lay a foundation other than the one which is laid, which is Jesus Christ," that Jesus is pictured as the foundation of the church. Nevertheless, in Ephesians 2:20, we read of the apostolic foundation: "having been built upon the foundation of the apostles and prophets, Christ Jesus Himself being the corner stone." First Peter 2:6-8 also pictures Jesus as the "corner stone." Revelation 21:14 speaks of the twelve foundation stones with the names of the apostles on them, "The wall of the city had twelve foundation stones, and on them were the twelve names of the twelve apostles of the Lamb." There is no contradiction in these texts; we simply must interpret each of them in their own context and understand their intent. Matthew's purpose (16:18) was to declare Christ's intention to build a new community upon the foundation of the apostles.[4]

The Identity: "My Church"

It helps to know who we are. As children, we were taught such essentials as our names, our parents' names, addresses, and telephone numbers. These were essential facts because they established self-identity and provided aid if we were ever lost. We can go a step further in this matter of identity. Psychologists speak often about knowing who we are or developing a strong self-identity. Perhaps my high school coach was somewhat of an amateur psychologist. My football team had established a great reputation as a football power in the piedmont region of North Carolina. During my junior year we won the state Triple-A crown. As the coach gave us our jackets with the championship title emblazoned, he warned us about the need to live up to our name not only on the field but off. "You're champions, so act like it." Could it be that the church today is sometimes ineffective because we are suffering from an identify crisis? Do we understand our true biblical identity?

The word that is translated "church" in the English Bible is from the Greek word *ekklēsia*. A Greek translation of the Old Testament, called the Septuagint, uses *ekklēsia* to translate a Hebrew word that means "congregation" or "community."

Literally it means a "called-out people." It was a most appropriate term for the Messiah to use to describe His messianic community. In Jewish thinking it would have been anticipated that the Messiah would develop a messianic community. This immediately suggests that the church has a direct sense of continuity with Old Testament Israel. The church is not some new invention; it was ordained in the heart of God, shadowed in direct continuity with Old Testament Israel, and now revealed, founded, and empowered in Christ Jesus. *Isaiah – remnant*

What is unique and striking here is the bold identification: *My* church. In this identification there is a clear and unmistakable claim to messiahship. The "people of God" had become the "people of the Messiah." The messianic task in a sense is to be focused in this community of purified and called-out people. Do you understand the obvious implications? We are His messianic community! Built by Him on the apostolic witness! The empowering and the ministry of the Messiah is tied up in us. We give visible expression to His rule on earth. The church is not a physical building, nor an ethnic group of people, nor even a particular denomination; rather, the church is a covenant people in fellowship with Christ, empowered for the redemption of the world.

It's Vitality: "I Will Build"

The metaphor of building already has been suggested by the imagery of the foundation rock. In Christ's declaration "I will build," there is an implicit promise of growth, progress, and vitality. We were founded not to be a static institution but a continually expanding building—or to change images—a growing organism.

All of us enjoy watching the progress of a building under construction. When a builder starts a new home in our neighborhood, our family enjoys riding or walking by on regular intervals to observe the progress. A few years back I began to watch with fascination as signs were erected announcing a new office building to be constructed on the Norfolk waterfront. Each week as I made my hospital rounds, I would look forward to driving past the construction area. During the first months there was really nothing to see. Huge, steam-powered pile drivers pounded pilings deep into the ground. The nature of the soil and the size of the building required a substantial foundation. Literally millions of dollars were spent on the foundation for this building. Now suppose I were to have driven by this site some months later only to discover that they had erected a single-story metal building on that expensive foundation. Wouldn't that have been surprising, confusing, and disappointing? Sure it would. It would be ridiculous to spend millions on a foundation to erect a small shed on it. God's intention in establishing a community on the foundation of the apostles with His Son as "corner stone" and builder was to erect a mighty community, a church triumphant—not a struggling, defeated, and powerless people.

Jesus' promise to build the church is a supernatural promise. We may provide programming, organize outreach, and keep records of the growth, but let us never forget that the growth of the body is supernatural. It is God's design and purpose for the church. When we are in a difficult situation and we hear about church growth, we often become somewhat defensive. I know because I've been there. It's true that God builds different churches in different ways according to the needs of the community. It's equally true that not every church is intended to be a megachurch. But we must quit making excuses for our lack of growth! We must abandon our defensiveness and learn to appreciate our diversity. We must allow God to build His church through us. Your church can grow! There are people to reach, and Christ has promised that He will build it. We are His called-out people!

Its Eternality: "Gates of Hell"

"It will build My church; and the gates of Hades shall not overpower it." Exactly what is meant by this powerful pictorial imagery? Some people interpret the gates of hell as representing the strength of Satan in this world. They picture the church as a fortress standing against the forces of evil. Evil is on the offensive, but the Christians are safe inside the church, and evil cannot overpower the church. Yet many object that this interpretation places the church on a defensive posture, as if Christians are huddled inside a walled fort while evil casts its assault against the church.

Those who object argue that gates do not move; therefore, the church is on the offensive against the powers of evil pictured as the "gates of Hades." They see the church on the offensive moving out into a world permeated by evil. The church triumphant is literally snatching folks from the very gates of hell. This latter picture is certainly more to our liking, and it is a true statement about the church. However, "gates of Hades" and similar expressions in other biblical references (Job 17:16; 38:17; Ps. 9:13; 107:18; and Isa. 38:10) refer to "death and dying." Look, for example, at Isaiah 38:10 that tells us about King Hezekiah who had just recovered from a life-threatening illness: "I said, 'in the middle of my life I am to enter the gates of Sheol; I am to be deprived of the rest of my years?"

When Jesus declared that the "gates of Hades shall not overpower" the church, He was asserting that the powers of death would not prevail against this community. Simply put, the church will not die! This community will last forever. We might call it God's Forever Family. There are many implications of this great truth. Those things that we do in the context of the church last forever. This puts a new light on changing diapers in preschool, working on a committee, or teaching in Sunday School. Our service here has eternal significance. It further tells us that friendships established here are eternal. This should encourage us concerning the fellowship of our churches.

Its Authority: "Keys of the Kingdom"

"I will give you the keys." Keys have had a certain fascination for all of us. We see babies entertaining themselves with their jingling sound. As children grow older they begin to understand the significance of a key. It will lock and unlock specified items such as doors. At about age nine or ten, children begin to desire a "key of my own." "I need my own key to the house in case I come home and no one is here." We decline because we know they'll lose the keys sooner or later. We try to explain that there is a certain level of responsibility involved in possessing keys. Finally, we decide to give in and give them keys suspended on cheap silver chains that probably will turn their necks green. Having hurdled this first barrier with keys, the next one comes when children turn sixteen. "Dad, I need my own keys to the car." You see our children recognize that keys symbolize authority. It is a more difficult lesson that keys also involve responsibility. When our children are issued their first speeding tickets and we take away the keys, they confront the matter of responsibility. The church must learn that "keys" mean authority and responsibility.

Not only were Peter and the disciples given a leading role in the foundation of the community, they also were given the authority to accomplish their work. Although this statement is technically still a part of the address to Peter, the authority symbolized by the "keys" was exercised by all the apostles. In fact, this authority of the "keys" came to be exercised by the church as a whole, as can be clearly seen in Matthew 18:15-20.

But, you ask, just what is meant by the symbol of the "keys"? There is widespread agreement that "authority" is the primary emphasis taught by the "keys." Yet scholars are somewhat evenly divided on the nature of the authority. Some argue that the authority is that of a steward who regulates administration. Others see the "keys" as the symbol of a porter who controls admission. These two ideas, in my mind, are not mutually exclusive. The words *loosing* and *binding* place the emphasis on admission, but even this is an element of the administrative task of the church. The authority of the "keys" truly belongs to the Son, but He places this sacred trust in the stewardship of the disciples, who at this time constituted His new community. The authority was not Peter's alone, but belongs to the church as a whole.

What authority then does the church exercise when we "bind" and "loose" persons by the "keys" placed in our stewardship. Don Carson pointed out that we can receive substantial help in understanding the authority of the keys by looking at Jesus' denunciation of the teachers of the law in Luke 11:52.[5] "Woe to you lawyers! For you have taken away the key of knowledge; you did not enter in yourselves, and those who were entering in you hindered." Notice that the teachers of the law had taken away the "key of knowledge." In doing so they failed themselves to enter into salvation, and, in turn, they prevented others from entering.

Peter, in contrast to the lawyers, confessed Jesus as Messiah and was told that he had been given the keys of the kingdom. The "keys" are simply, but profoundly, the "gospel [good news] of the kingdom," which Jesus Himself had been declaring (Matt. 4:23). Peter and the disciples, by way of revelation, confessed they believed that Jesus was the fulfillment of the

gospel. Now by proclaiming this truth, they opened the kingdom to those who would believe and shut it to those who would
not respond.

This interpretation fits the entire scheme of Matthew's Gospel and points out the significance of this passage. In Matthew
4:19 we are told that Jesus called the disciples to be fishers of
men. In Matthew 10, this calling is further elaborated in terms
of preaching the good news of the kingdom. Notice, too, that
in chapter 10 there is a clear connection between the message
declared by the disciples and the binding and loosing of persons. In verse 40, Jesus declared, "He who receives you receives Me, and he who receives Me receives Him who sent
Me." He further warned them that this message would "loose"
others: "Do not think that I came to bring peace on the earth;
I did not come to bring peace, but a sword" (10:34). In Matthew 16:13-20 the message of redemption is fully revealed in
Jesus who is God's Messiah. This truth is the key that determines the eternal destiny of those who will hear it. This fully
prepares us for the commissioning of the church to go into all
nations and present the gospel (Matt. 28:19-20). Thus Matthew
16:13-20 is pivotal for understanding the flow of Matthew's
Gospel and the purpose of the church. The church has been
called out to declare the redemptive work of God through
Jesus the Messiah.

This same truth is fleshed out in the first chapters of the Book
at Acts. In Acts 2:14-42 we discover Peter's great Pentecost
sermon. He declared to His listeners the good news "of the
kingdom," then called them to decision: "Repent, and let each
of you be baptized in the name of Jesus Christ for the forgiveness of your sins; . . . So then, those who had received his word
were baptized; and there were added that day about three
thousand souls" (2:38, 41). We could say that those who responded were bound by the "keys of the kingdom."

In Acts 4:11-12 we encounter the loosing function of the
keys. Peter declared the message of Jesus Christ before the
Sanhedrin. He declared that Jesus was the stone that was rejected by the Jews, yet He was the very "corner stone." Notice
Peter's conclusion: "There is salvation in no one else; for there
is no other name under heaven that has been given among
men, by which we must be saved" (Acts 4:12). To reject the
witness to the "corner stone" of redemption is to loose oneself,

for there is no other door of redemption. The binding and the loosing then is accomplished by the preaching of the gospel that has already been given.

The verbs translated "shall be bound" and "shall be loosed" (Matt. 16:19, KJV) are in the future perfect tense. They could literally be translated "shall have been bound" and "shall have been loosed." It is not that heaven belatedly ratifies decisions made by Peter or the apostles. Rather, the church gives visible expression to decisions already sanctioned in heaven. We should not lose sight of the fact that the decisions made in the life of the church are eternal in nature. There is an *inextricable* link between life-changing commitments and the decisions expressed in the church fellowship. As long as we adhere to and declare the gospel, we exercise the authority of binding and loosing because heaven has already acted on this matter.

Several significant implications can be drawn from these truths. We can never grow casual or indifferent toward personal spiritual decisions that occur in the life of our fellowship. Whether it is a school-age child or a senior adult, it is a decision that is eternal. It is not just a matter of it being "nice" that we're reaching senior adults or youth, but it is the fact that the decisions made in our midst will determine where these folks will spend eternity.

Second, we must think of decisions made by the body of Christ itself. I'm referring to those business decisions about paving parking lots, painting hallways, paying staff, and so forth. We must never address these issues in a coolly calculated business manner without the recognition that the church is dealing with eternity. Many a church's witness to its community has been affected by the way it conducts its business. We must make these decisions in light of our authority and responsibility to be stewards of the "keys of the kingdom."

Third, we must address the current-day apathy that afflicts so many churches—church leaders begging for volunteers to teach our children, a constant lack of funds, and people who attend when it suits their schedule. With so much at stake, how can we tolerate apathy? If you were elected to sit on a committee of our government whose work would determine world peace, how would you approach your work? Would you attend when it was convenient? Would you allow scheduling conflicts to take precedence over your commitment to serve on this committee? Certainly you wouldn't! Too much would be at stake! This passage confronts us with an unavoidable truth. More is at stake in the work of the church than in the committee meetings in the buildings of Washington, D.C. While legislators may deal with life and death, war and peace, we deal with heaven and hell and eternity itself. When we confess Jesus as our Savior and Lord, we make a priority commitment to accept both the "authority" and "responsibility" of the "keys of the kingdom of heaven."

4. Finally, we must address the matter of evangelistic outreach and the modern-day church. I hear many church leaders speak of evangelism as one facet of our work. This has often caused many pastors and laypersons to consider evangelistic outreach as an optional ministry.[6] They say, "This is a task we'll leave to the professional evangelists or to other churches." If we are called to exercise the authority of the keys, we must be active in declaring the good news. This is an unavoidable conclusion. Evangelism must penetrate all we do in the life of the church. We must reach out to embrace the lost world in the name of Christ. Like the children playing Red Rover, our task is not done until we have "bound" all within our power to reach. It is God's desire that not one would perish. This is *no game.*

Notes

1. R. T. France, *Matthew*, Tyndale New Testament Commentary (Grand Rapids: Wm. B. Eerdman, 1985), 254. Dick France argued that *Petros* (or in the underlying Aramaic *Cephas*) was an original choice by Jesus. He found no other use of this as a name prior to that time.

2. D. A. Carson, *Matthew*, vol. 8 in *The Expositor's Bible Commentary* (Grand Rapids: Zondervan Publishing House, 1984), 368.

3. For further insight, see Don Carson's excellent argument concerning this matter: Ibid., 367-369.

4. We see a similar concept where in certain contexts the church is discussed as the body of Christ composed of a variety of members that function like eyes, ears, and other body parts (1 Cor. 12). In other contexts the body imagery depicts Christ as the head of the body. Again there is no contradiction, simply a different emphasis.

5. Ibid., 373. Don Carson's entire presentation of this matter deserves study, 370-373.

6. See *Growing an Evangelistic Sunday School* by Kenneth Hemphill and Wayne Jones (Nashville: Broadman Press, 1989).

3

Freeze Tag

For this reason I too, having heard of the faith in the Lord Jesus which exists among you, and your love for all the saints, do not cease giving thanks for you, while making mention of you in my prayers; that the God of our Lord Jesus Christ, the Father of glory, may give to you a spirit of wisdom and of revelation in the knowledge of Him. I pray that the eyes of your heart may be enlightened, so that you may know what is the hope of His calling, what are the riches of the glory of His inheritance in the saints, and what is the surpassing greatness of His power toward us who believe. These are in accordance with the working of the strength of His might which He brought about in Christ, when He raised Him from the dead, and seated Him at His right hand in the heavenly places, far above all rule and authority and power and dominion, and every name that is named, not only in this age, but also in the one to come. And He put all things in subjection under His feet, and gave Him as head over all things to the church, which is His body, the fulness of Him who fills all in all.

—Ephesians 1:15-23

Got you! Freeze! Familiar words to all those who have played freeze tag. Freeze tag is a simple variation of the basic game of tag. Usually it is played by five or six children in a limited playing field—most often a backyard. The individual who is "it" chases and tags the other participants. When a person is tagged, he or she must "freeze" where tagged. The "frozen" player can't move for the duration of the game unless "thawed" by one of the players who has not yet been tagged and frozen.

It appears that many churches in our nation have been frozen in place. They've been stationary in most areas of ministry. Membership and attendance have been stable for years, and they're likely to remain that way for the forseeable future unless something happens to the community surrounding the church.

Why have they become frozen and thus stationary? That's a

good question to which there are no sure and absolute answers to cover every situation. Some, perhaps, have been frozen by a poor self-image. They have grown to believe that they can't grow. They can't reach their community! They can't do anymore than they are doing now. They simply have been brainwashed into believing they're doing all they can do to reach their community. Some churches have been frozen because of sheer apathy or fatigue. Sometimes while playing freeze tag children get so tired avoiding being tagged that they just give up and allow themselves to be frozen. Some church leaders appear to have grown tired of trying to develop the enthusiasm to recruit and train the leaders necessary to grow a church.

I think some other churches have been frozen because they have become content with what they are now doing. They've reached a "good size" according to their own thinking. They have enough people to pay the bills and hire an extra staff member to entertain the youth. They have all they need. They're comfortable in their frozen position, so it's just easier not to move.

I sense that many of these churches that have been frozen—whatever the reason—long to be thawed and to move again. In freeze tag, one can be thawed only when touched by another participant and freed from icy bondage. Likewise, only as we are touched by the hand of God can the church be freed to move once again. The greatest need of our day is for the church to recapture the vision of what it is called to be and thus to fully realize its own potential.

Our own potential may be one of the most difficult realities that we face every morning of our lives. Most of us recognize that we rarely live up to our potential. We simply do not push ourselves to excellence in many areas of life.

Early in my pastoral ministry, I used to spend my August afternoons visiting the practice sessions of our local high school football team. Having played in college, I would sometimes find myself a willing recruit to help with the kickers or linebackers. Occasionally, I would come across a guy with incredible ability. I mean this guy had "star" written all over him and potential oozing out of every pore. All too frequently these individuals with vast potential only wanted to do enough to "get by." They simply could not be stimulated to perform to their own best standards, to fully utilize the gifts that were theirs. I can remember how frustrating this was in our coaches' meetings. "Doesn't this kid realize what gifts he has? How can we help him understand what a tragedy it is to waste such gifts?"

We must turn these same questions toward the spiritual dimension. Do we corporately, as the body of Christ, understand what has been made available to us in Christ? Have we even begun to come to grips with our dynamic potential? On an even more personal level, are you living up to your spiritual potential? Are you fully utilizing your gifts in service to the body of Christ?

We have already discovered that after the daring confession, "You are the Christ [Messiah], the Son of the living God," Jesus revealed His plan to build His messianic community. This new congregation would have as its foundation the apostolic witness to God's Messiah. It would be a dynamic community given supernatural power because Christ Himself would be the builder. The messianic community would embrace eternity because even the "gates of hell" (Matt. 16:18, KJV), death itself, would not overcome it. Finally, functioning on earth as the steward of the "keys of the kingdom," heaven and hell would be at stake in its operations and ministries. What incredible opportunity, responsibility, and potential.

Yet when we look at many of the local churches we have known about or attended, we seldom see much of this potential realized. Occasionally, we wonder if such an empowering will ever be experienced in the church to which we belong. After years of disappointment, we grow accustomed to excusing our lack of growth and ministry based on circumstances like our location, lack of funds, or leadership. We must come clean here! If the church is Christ's body and He is her builder, then we have far more potential than we have even begun to realize. Too much is at stake not to strive to live up to our potential.

The Ephesian Letter

While many of Paul's letters deal with the potential of the church, Ephesians is the letter that challenges us to throw off our apathy and become what we are empowered to be. This letter was composed in a prison cell along with Colossians.

They are companion letters and should be studied together. Epaphras, a leader in the church at Colossae, had come to Paul out of deep concern for the Christians in Colossae, Laodicea, and Hierapolis (Col. 4:12-13). From the content of Colossians we can determine that Epaphras must have been concerned over heretical teachings that were spreading throughout proconsular Asia.

This heresy is difficult to name. Some of the correctives we find in Colossians and Ephesians suggest that the ideas being taught were germinal ideas that later were developed into a system of teaching we call gnosticism. Central to our study is the fact that the heretical teachings included a strange combination of Jewish and pagan elements that made much of the spiritual powers in the universe (read Col. 2:8-23). Gnosticism was eclectic enough to make room for Christ in its scheme of salvation, but it denied His supremacy and His uniqueness in the redemptive work of God. (Similarities with the so-called New Age movement of our day are striking.) As we might anticipate, when Christ was not seen as the unique Son of God, then the church that claimed His name would be viewed as nothing more than another religious sect, not unlike the countless mystery religions of that day. Notice once again that the uniqueness of Christ and the uniqueness of the church are bound together. This truth was made clear in our study of Matthew 16:13-20.

In Colossians Paul confronted the troubling heretical teachings straight on. In the Ephesian letter, intended to be shared with the churches of proconsular Asia, Paul in a more contemplative and prayerful mood addressed the full range of issues that emerged from the winds of heretical teaching swirling through proconsular Asia. Paul's conviction was sure. Christ is uniquely God's Son, and therefore He is the very fullness of God. Even more profound is the church, His body, is therefore invested with vast potential and strength because of its union with Christ.

Ephesians 1: The Context

In Ephesians 1 Paul began with a moving description of the blessings of redemption experienced by the individual believer. Just glancing through those first verses brings us face-to-face with some of the most wonderful promises of the Bible.

verse 3: "[God] has blessed us with every spiritual blessing in the heavenly places in Christ."

verse 4: "He chose us in Him before the foundation of the world, that we should be holy and blameless before Him."

verse 5: "He predestined us to adoption as sons through Jesus Christ to Himself."

verses 7-8: "In Him we have *redemption* through His blood, the forgiveness of our trespasses, according to the riches of His grace, which He lavished upon us" (author's italics).

verses 9-10: "He made known to us the mystery of His will, . . . the summing up of all things in Christ."

verse 11: "In Him also we have obtained an inheritance."

We simply cannot ignore phrases like "in love," "kind intention of His will," "freely bestowed," "lavished upon us," and "riches of His grace." The sense of personal love and fullness of redemption could not be clearer. These blessings occurred according to the purpose of God established before the foundation of the world (v. 4). Now by listening to the message of truth, the gospel of salvation, and believing, we can be sealed in Him by the power of the Holy Spirit (v. 13). Because we now have our existence "in Him," we can participate in the full range of blessings that are in Christ. The full redemption of our bodies still remains (see Rom. 8:23), and thus suffering and sickness still exist. Yet we are assured of His fullness by the pledge of the Spirit Himself. (v. 14).

In verse 14 a subtle shading begins that places our individual heritage in the context of the church. The Holy Spirit is the down payment of "our inheritance." The possessive pronoun "our" includes all believers, whether they be Jew or Gentile. Together we are the redeemed possession of God. While our response to the gospel is a personal and individual decision, our salvation necessarily involves us in the life of the community as a whole. We thus are sealed by the Spirit in community. Our incorporation into the community, which is God's possession, means that we are involved in His redemptive work. Because of this great truth Paul literally bursts into prayer for the church: "For this reason I too, having heard of the faith in the Lord Jesus which exists among you, and your love for all the saints, do not cease giving thanks for you, while making mention of you in my prayers" (vv. 15-16).

Notice first that Paul primarily prayed that these Christians would come to understand what was already theirs by inheritance. They needed both wisdom and spiritual understanding to grasp these great truths. They cannot be comprehended by the non-Christian because they come by way of divine revelation. The combination of knowledge and wisdom is significant. Wisdom is the God-given ability to utilize the spiritual knowledge one gains by revelation. Paul was not urging them toward the sheer accumulation of facts for the simple love of knowledge, but he was pressing them to a personal knowledge that would alter their total life-style. Paul was, in fact, wanting them to possess that personal knowledge of God that was the very quest of his own life: "That I may know Him, and the power of His resurrection and the fellowship of His sufferings" (Phil. 3:10).

So often we fail to realize our potential because we fail to understand what is available to us. I don't know how you went about taking exams when you were in school. I was one of the eager-beaver types. As soon as the test paper hit my desk, I frantically tried to answer the questions as quickly as possible. I guess I had crammed so hard that I was sure I couldn't contain all that information very long, so I just let it gush out quickly. Upon inquiry, most people tell me they followed a similar procedure. Did you ever take a test that was so demanding that it seemed to require a thorough knowledge of the entire textbook? You found yourself sitting there agonizing to retrieve all the bits of information that you had stored up over the entire semester. You left the class drained and sure that you had performed poorly. You were eager to find someone to see if they had as much difficulty as you.

"Boy, that was a tough exam. I can't believe anyone could expect us to recall all that information. I'm sure I flunked! How did you do?"

"What do you mean, hard? I thought it was pretty easy! Anytime we have an open book test I know I can do well."

"Open book? You're kidding!"

"Didn't you read the directions? Didn't you use the book? No wonder you found it hard. Without the book it would have been impossible."

If we don't understand all the resources available to us on a particular exam or project, we are not likely to do well. In like manner, if we fail to understand all that is available to us in

Christ, we must certainly fail to realize our potential individually and corporately. Let's look together at Paul's prayer. Even on our first reading we will note that it is a prayer for threefold knowledge that embraces eternity, past, present, and future.

The Hope of His Calling

The source of all true hope for believers and for the church is found in the calling of God. Notice that Paul wrote "the hope of His calling," not "your" calling (v. 18). With this phrase we are hurled backward to the past of eternity itself. The hope of His calling finds its origin in the plan of God, before the foundation of the world. We looked briefly at this great truth in verses 3-14, and the content of those verses summarizes the truth of "His calling." We are God's chosen people—chosen in Christ before the foundation on the world (v. 4). This choice becomes effective and active when we respond to the gospel and believe in Him (v. 13). Yet His calling and His plan for His people were determined before the world was formed. "His calling" is in His Son, and the sure hope of His promise is that we will be the recipients of the spiritual blessings detailed in verses 3-14. While in this life, we are continually being transformed into the image of His Son. In the final consummation we will be glorified with Christ. We thus are called to live out the implications of "His calling," that the world would see in us the clear evidence of the working of God.

This idea is fleshed out somewhat more specifically in chapter 3. In the first verses of that chapter, Paul told of his great joy in being the recipient of a great mystery that had been hidden in other generations but had now been made known through the holy apostles and prophets (3:4-5). That mystery is nothing less than the church itself made up of Jew and Gentile alike. Paul had been gifted to minister to this church and to proclaim to the Gentiles in particular "the unfathomable riches of Christ, and to bring to light what is the administration of the mystery which for ages has been hidden in God, who created all things; in order that the manifold wisdom of God might now be made known through the church to the rulers and authorities in the heavenly places" (3:8-10).[1] Are you beginning to understand "His calling?" We are called to be a company of redeemed persons who display to the world, and even to the spiritual powers, the wisdom of God. This is our calling—our hope—our purpose.

I sometimes am amused by folks who try to suggest that Christianity and thus the church are of rather recent origin. They argue that other world religions or eastern beliefs are much older than Christianity. They thus imply that their ancient origin makes them more original or authentic than Christianity. The truth is the church was in the heart of God before the foundation of the world. You can't get any more ancient or authentic than that!

The Riches of His Inheritance (v. 18)

Once again you should notice that it is *His* "inheritance in the saints" and not *our* inheritance. Paul previously spoke of our inheritance (vv. 11,14), but this is something far more grand. This picks up an Old Testament image of God's inheritance being in "His people." For example, in Deuteronomy 32:9 we read, "For the Lord's portion is His people;/Jacob is the allotment of His inheritance." That entire passage deserves your attention in relationship to understanding the richness of the church as His inheritance. In verse 10 the writer mentions God's care for Jacob. He compared God's love to that of a mother eagle's care for her young (v. 11). He draws our attention to the guidance of the Lord (v. 12) and His abundant provision for "His inheritance."

Now we are asked to fathom a great truth. We together as believers constitute an inheritance for God. We are His own possession in whom He desires to display to the universe His manifold wisdom (3:10). Here we get a small glimpse of what joy it must give to God our Father when He sees us fulfill His purpose and reflect His glory.

As I was contemplating this passage, a scene from my childhood kept coming to memory that helped me to understand this truth. I began playing little league baseball when I was nine years old. My first year coincided with the first year of little league ball for our community. I'm not sure there is any correlation, but it seemed to me that everyone who went out for the various teams were huge in comparison to my tiny nine-year-old frame. Somehow I ended up behind the plate and became the starting catcher. I had good hand-eye coordination and little trouble in the defensive portion of the game.

Offense was another matter. The pitchers looked towering as they took their positions on the mound only sixty feet away. I think I set a record for strikeouts that year. For some reason, I never really developed into a very good hitter during those little league years. As I got older and larger, it became a source of embarrassment that I had never hit a home run. Most of my friends had several home runs to their credit.

I'll never forget the steamy July night that I finally got my pitch and lined a shot for the center field fence. It's unimportant that my home run bounded off the top of the fence. It got over, and that's all that counted. Running the bases was a blur. The crowd, a hundred or so, was going wild. I was on a cloud. As I rounded third and headed for home I could see only one face in the stands behind the plate. It was my dad. His face reflected my joy and my achievement one hundred times over. I sensed that this meant far more to him than it did to me. It was as if he had hit the home run. I couldn't understand it at the time, but now that I'm a parent it is much more clear. Nothing gives me greater joy than watching one of my three girls perform to their potential. I share in that glory. Now we are His inheritance! What joy it must give God when the church performs according to its potential.

The Surpassing Greatness of His Power

First we looked at God's call that took us back to the days before the foundation of the earth. Then we focused on "His inheritance" that caused us to visualize God's purpose for the church in the coming consummation. These are wonderful and moving truths. But the zenith of this prayer is found in the request that we would know the surpassing greatness of God's power in the present. In the Greek we often find the "rule of end stress," which means that the idea being emphasized is placed last in the sentence. These events were taken out of the normal sequence (past, present, and future) in order to underline this great truth concerning our present empowering. We are often guilty of dwelling in the past of our salvation or the future of our heavenly home and failing to realize our potential in the present. Paul desired that we avoid this ever-present dilemma.

Our minds boggle as we try to comprehend power in any form. As children we were fascinated by television superheros who exhibited superhuman strength. This fascination continued unabated into our youth and young adult years as we idolized athletes who displayed great physical strength. As adults we often envy the power of those who climb the corporate ladder of success. Power and strength fascinate us. We are both frightened and intrigued by the power of the wind and waves in a storm. We find it difficult to comprehend various forms of mechanical or electrical power, but we seek to harness them. The power unleashed in the splitting of the atom is simply beyond imagination. I remember my first visit aboard a nuclear powered aircraft carrier in Norfolk. I was like a wide-eyed child as the officer conducting the tour explained that the mammoth vessel could cruise around the world on a few handfuls of atomic fuel. What vast power!

Yet the power that Paul spoke of is beyond all these forms of power. It is the power of God Himself: the power that brought life in the event of creation, the power that could hold back the waters of the Red Sea or destroy the walls of Jericho, and the very power that could raise Jesus from the dead and exalt Him to the right hand of the Father. Wonder of wonders! This is the power "toward us who believe" (v. 19).

Many of the wonderful truths of God's love are simply difficult to put into words. This power is one of those truths. Paul attempted to describe this power in the strongest terms possible by using the phrase "surpassing greatness of His power" and by stacking four synonyms for power, one on top of the other. These four words are translated as "power," "working," "strength, and "might" in the *New American Standard Bible.* The word translated "power" is the Greek *dunamis* from which we get our word *dynamite.* "Working" comes from the Greek *energeia,* from which the English word *energy* is derived. This power was not just an abstract concept for Paul, but is is experienced in the working of God's might.

Now Paul moved to the single greatest illustration of that power. The resurrection of Jesus from the dead was not only the acknowledgment of Jesus as Lord of all, it was a supreme manifestation of the Father's power. The ascension of Jesus to the right hand of the Father bestows upon the Son the highest possible honor (see Phil. 2:9-11), and itself demonstrates the mighty power of God.

But please don't miss the point of this whole section. The

resurrection and the ascension of Jesus express the measure of the power made available to the church. Notice this same idea stated in Ephesians 3:20, "Now to Him who is able to do exceeding abundantly beyond all that we ask or think, according to the power that works within us." You'll recall Paul expressed the hunger of his heart in the phrase "that I may know Him, and the power of His resurrection" (Phil. 3:10). This is the power that not only gives new life to persons dead in sin, but also it animates and empowers the church for service in this present age. This is the power experienced in the life of the church—the body of Christ. Only when we fully discover what we are a part of can we begin to live it out in daily ministry. The church today is often like the children of Israel on the edge of the Promised Land. They had vast potential before them—theirs for the taking—and they still thought like slaves.

The thought of the resurrection and ascension leads to the further truth that Christ is Lord of all. He is "far above all rule and authority and power and dominion" (v. 21). The words in this verse possibly reflect titles of spiritual powers that were worshiped by the false teachers in proconsular Asia. We find a similar listing in Colossians 1:16, "For by Him all things were created, both in the heavens and on earth, visible and invisible, whether thrones or dominions or rulers or authorities—all things have been created by Him and for Him." There is little value in trying to find some sort of spiritual ranking in these various titles, for the truth of this verse is abundantly clear. Jesus Christ is Lord over every spiritual power. The phrase "every name that is named" (Eph. 1:21) probably refers to any spiritual power ever reverenced by human beings. No matter, Christ is Lord. In the cross, resurrection, and ascension, He has defeated them all (Col. 2:15; see Rom. 8:38). During this present age of the church, we may still have to do battle with these spiritual forces (Eph. 6:12), but we do so in the power of the One who is Lord. God's plan for the church is to demonstrate to these spiritual powers the manifold wisdom of Himself (Eph. 3:10).

In a world searching for wisdom and salvation through horoscopes, tea leaves, Ouija boards, fortune tellers, channeling, and bogus hopes for reincarnation, we have a message. Christ is Lord! He alone is the answer. He alone can bring salvation.

But our challenge as the church is to demonstrate the great power that is available to us.

The Bottom Line

What does all this mean? What is the bottom line? "He put all things in subjection under His feet, and gave Him as head over all things *to the church*" (author's italics). By virtue of His exaltation and by the divine appointment of His Father, Christ is the supreme head of the church. Note that our head is head over all things. Can you comprehend what authority that gives to the church? Our authority and power are derived from Him who is our head. Can you hear the echoes of Jesus' promise? "I will build My church; and the gates of Hades shall not overpower it" (Matt. 16:18). That promise was sealed by His resurrection and ascension.

Paul used the imagery of the body in several distinct ways to picture the church. In 1 Corinthians 12, the head is simply another member of the body. Paul's concern in that letter was to encourage unity in diversity. Here the head is not simply a part of the body, but it is Christ Himself. The head denotes that He is supreme Lord. It implies our total dependence upon Him and the need for total submission and obedience to Him. Further, it declares our essential union with Him. The imagery is much the same as that of the vine and the branches in John 15:5. He is the living whole, and we have life and strength only as His power flows through us. As His body, we carry out His mission and purpose in this world. This is empowering for service and is experienced in obedience to our Lord.

J. Armitage Robinson, a great biblical scholar of a past generation, called the phrase "the fulness of Him who fills all in all" the most remarkable expression in the whole epistle.[2] Simply paraphrased, the church should be the full expression of Jesus Christ who Himself fills everything. The Greek term *fullness* (*plērōma*) has a wide range of meanings in the New Testament. Here the sense seems to be that the church is intended to receive and express in the world the fullness of Him who fills all in all.[3] As Christ is the full expression of the Godhead (see Col. 1:19; 2:9), so the church is called to be the full expression of Christ. In Ephesians 4:10-12, Paul picked up this same theme in reference to the exalted Christ who gifts the church: "He who descended is Himself also He who ascended far above all the heavens, that He might fill all things. And He gave some as apostles, and some as prophets, and some as evangelists, and some as pastors and teachers, for the equipping of the saints for the work of service." We have here a biblical promise that the church will receive the full empowering and gifts to express Christ to the world.

What magnificent potential is ours. What an awesome responsibility. The church can have no place for apathy, no room for fearful cringing when the world has such need, no place for weak excuses. The church is not a game but a spiritual fortress.

We have been "frozen" by our own failures. The Spirit of the living God desires to touch us and "thaw" us once again for dynamic service and growth. We are His, and He is Lord of all. We must begin to live up to our potential.

Notes

1. We will return to this passage in greater detail in the next chapter.

2. J. Armitage Robinson, *Commentary on Ephesians* (Grand Rapids: Kregel Publications, 1979; first published 1903), 42.

3. Some commentators take this phrase in the sense that the church fills or completes Christ. I do not find the arguments for this interpretation very convincing. If Christ is the fullness of God, the church can in no way complete or fill Him.

4

From Check to Checkmate

As a result, we are no longer to be children, tossed here and there by waves, and carried about by every wind of doctrine, by the trickery of men, by craftiness in deceitful scheming; but speaking the truth in love, we are to grow up in all aspects into Him, who is the head, even Christ, from whom the whole body, being fitted and held together by that which every joint supplies, according to the proper working of each individual part, causes the growth of the body for the building up of itself in love.

This I say therefore, and affirm together with the Lord, that you walk no longer just as the Gentiles also walk, in the futility of their mind, being darkened in their understanding, excluded from the life of God, because of the ignorance that is in them, because of the hardness of their heart; and they, having become callous, have given themselves over to sensuality, for the practice of every kind of impurity with greediness. But you did not learn Christ in this way, if indeed you have heard Him and have been taught in Him, just as truth is in Jesus.

—Ephesians 4:14-21

The game of chess has always intrigued me. I've never had the patience to learn all the intricacies of this game. I've played enough to know how the different pieces move. I know, too, that the ultimate goal is to capture the opponent's king. When the game is nearing completion and you believe that you have your opponent in a situation where you can win in another move, you must call "check." At this point you are convinced you have the potential for victory, but you haven't won yet. Your opponent has one turn to move his king out of danger or "check." It is not impossible that the game can continue from this point for several more moves. There are times that the opponent may rally from this difficult position of being in "check" and actually win the match. It is often difficult to move from "check" to "checkmate," that is, to move from having the potential to win to winning in reality.

For many Christians and churches, this step from potential

victory to actual victory is a difficult one to make. How do we go from *understanding* who we are in Christ to *becoming* who we are in Christ? How do we move from *understanding* growth principles to *applying* growth principles in such a way that they actually work in our local situation? If, by virtue of the resurrection of Christ, we have been empowered to be "the fulness of Him who fills all in all" (1:23), we have everything necessary to move to checkmate. How do we then live up to our heritage, our empowering? Must we do so? I think this is one of the most critical challenges facing the church in the nineties. I would be so bold as to say that it is essential to the purpose of God in the world today that the church live up to its heritage!

How does that statement make you feel? Do you wonder if it's accurate? Some folks want to excuse human responsibility by overemphasizing the sovereignty of God. God can do what He wants with or without us! Sounds good, but is that the way God works? Do you shudder at the awesome responsibility of living up to our heritage in Christ? I know what you may be thinking: *If God has to depend on my church, things are in pretty bad shape.* Does that thought challenge you? We must understand and apply the truths of God's Word concerning our heritage.

I became convinced of the truth of the abundant power available to the church during my time of study in Cambridge, England. The rich heritage which is ours as the church continues to challenge and stimulate me as a pastor. It generates for me a deep level of enthusiasm and energy for my service through the church. Long hours of committee work, or the unheralded duties like mopping up leaks after a bad rainstorm, can become terribly frustrating if they are not viewed in light of our heritage and our responsibility.

To say that the church is essential to the purpose of God in the world today does not in any way depreciate the sovereign power of God. God has chosen throughout history to work through human instrumentation. It is both a privilege and a responsibility that He has chosen to work through the church "in order that the manifold wisdom of God might now be made known" (Eph. 3:10). To know that the sovereign, all-powerful God could use me—could use us—to work out His divine plan of redemption moves me to greater commitment.

You will recall that in the last chapter we looked at prayer for the churches of Asia Minor. Paul prayed that their eyes and hearts would be enlightened so that they could know (1) the hope of His calling, (2) the riches of His glory, and (3) the surpassing greatness of His power. The power made available to the church is the power that raised Jesus from the dead. Thus the church is to be the complete expression of God's fullness (see 1:18-23). In this chapter we're going to look at a second prayer in which Paul challenged his readers to live up to their high calling.

The Context

Our prayer is found in Ephesians 3, but it will be helpful to look at the immediate context first. In chapter 2 Paul discussed the marvelous truth of our personal redemption. He described our condition before our salvation very graphically.

> You were dead in your trespasses and sins, in which you formerly walked according to the course of this world, according to the prince of the power of the air, of the spirit that is now working in the sons of disobedience. Among them we too all formerly lived in the lusts of our flesh, indulging the desires of the flesh and of the mind, and were by nature children of wrath, even as the rest (Eph. 2:1-3).

But now by the grace of God those who were formerly children of wrath have been made sons of God. Notice too that this personal redemption broke down barriers that had divided groups like the Jews and the Gentiles and reconciled them in "one body to God" (v. 16). What Christ did in His body (His flesh) on the cross, He did for His body, the church. This great truth finds full expression in verse 19: "So then you are no longer strangers and aliens, but you are fellow citizens with the saints, and are of God's household." This household of God is the church spoken of by Jesus in Matthew 16. It is the new community built upon the apostles and prophets with Jesus as its cornerstone.

In the first verses of chapter 3 Paul wrote of his own calling and ministry. He had been privileged to understand and teach concerning a profound mystery that has only now been made known "to His holy apostles and prophets in the Spirit" (v. 5). Through revelation, Paul, as one of the New Testament apostles and prophets, had received full understanding of that which could be seen only partially and dimly by the "sons of men" of the past.

The Mystery of Christ

What then was the content of the revelation? What did Paul mean by "mystery of Christ"? Some commentators suggest that the content of the mystery is the inclusion of the Gentiles in the people of God. Yet even a cursory study of the Old Testament will show the reader that God has always intended that the Gentiles share in His divine blessings along with the Jews. This plan began with the call to Abraham in Genesis 12:3, "In you all the families of the earth shall be blessed." The Jews were called to be a blessing to other nations. Thus the inclusion of the Gentiles can hardly be the content of the mystery now revealed. What was not clearly seen by the "sons of men" was that "in Christ Jesus" the Gentiles and the Jews would be "one new man" (2:15), reconciled "in one body" (2:16), and that one body is the church. In this new community, Jew and Gentile would partake of God's grace in like manner as they responded to the gospel.

Notice the three compound words in 3:6: "fellow heirs," "fellow members," and "fellow partakers." Jew and Gentile are equally members of the one body. They both partake of the covenant promises "in Christ Jesus through the gospel." God had revealed this good news to Paul, and he had to share it with all people, particularly the Gentiles.

The truth concerning God's plan for a new *ekklesia,* made up of Jew and Gentile as fellow members, was so profound that Paul was overwhelmed by his role in declaring this truth. "To me, the very least of all saints, this grace was given, to preach to the Gentiles the unfathomable riches of Christ" (3:8). You may think this passage doesn't apply to you because you're not the apostle Paul or even an ordained minister. Others are reluctant to witness because they believe themselves to be unworthy. God's grace is so overwhelming we are all awed by His goodness. The truth is that we are all ministers, made worthy by God's mercy and empowered to serve by the grace given each of us. We all can declare that anyone—regardless of color, creed, or nationality—can experience the unfathomable riches of Christ and become a fellow member of His body, the church.

Paul's apostolic work among the Gentiles was a gift of grace. In the giving of the grace for ministry, God also gave Paul the power to accomplish His work. The word translated "working" is *energeia* from which we get the English word *energy*. *Power* translates *dunamis* from which we get *dynamic* and *dynamite*. (v. 7). The energizing power of God is available to us in Christ for service and witness in His body. We, like Paul, stand in awe as we struggle to comprehend the unsearchable riches of Christ who saves us, calls us, and empowers us to serve Him.

His Wisdom Through the Church

Paul readily confessed his awe at being called to preach to the Gentiles. He had been privileged to play a small part in the unveiling of the mystery of God concerning His new community. Now Paul moved to a truth he considered equally awesome. I use this word not in a colloquial sense but in a theological one. The truth Paul shared in verse 10 should inspire awe, reverence, and wonder in every believer. Just listen: "In order that the manifold wisdom of God might now be made known through the church to the rulers and the authorities in the heavenly places."

While the universe, the very creation of God, presents ample evidence of the power and glory of God, it is His church —the centerpiece of His new creation—that truly reveals the manifold wisdom of God. The picture that should come to mind is that of God the Father holding up His church, "His workmanship" (2:10), before all the rulers and authorities as a demonstration of His multifaceted wisdom.

We all enjoy demonstrating our workmanship. My youngest daughter is now eight years old, and I am the proud recipient of numerous works of art from her hand. She never tires of showing me what she has drawn, and I never grow weary of admiring her pictures. I think someone invented refrigerators just so we would have a special place to hang our children's pictures. When we have drawn or crafted something with our own hands, we take great joy in sharing it with others. Allow this truth to challenge you! The God of creation holds us, His church, up before all the spiritual powers of the universe as a demonstration of His great wisdom!

The phrase "the rulers and the authorities" (3:10) refers to spiritual powers both good and evil. Paul was saying that God is actually educating the spiritual powers by means of the church. Peter wrote that as God revealed His redemptive plan for humankind, the angels watched with rapt interest. Peter described salvation history as "things into which the angels long to look" (1 Pet. 1:12). In 1 Corinthians 11:10 Paul reprimanded the Corinthians about unseemly behavior by reminding them that the angels watched the activities of the church. The Lord Himself told us "there is joy in the presence of the angels of God over one sinner who repents" (Luke 15:10).

The angels themselves learn of the manifold wisdom of God through His new creation, the church. People sometimes look at the church and see only its weaknesses, its flaws, or its warts, and they discount it as foolish and insignificant. This shouldn't surprise us. Remember in the Corinthian letter Paul said the unsaved man would look at God's plan of salvation through "Christ crucified" and see it as foolishness. "But to those who are the called, both Jews and Greeks, Christ the power of God and the wisdom of God. Because the foolishness of God is wiser than men, and the weakness of God is stronger than men" (1 Cor. 1:24-25). In a manner similar to the cross, the church—while seemingly insignificant to the unsaved—in truth displays the manifold, many-colored beauty of God's wisdom.

One other thought is worthy of mention. The phrase "the rulers and the authorities" also includes the powers that oppose God. You'll recall that the demons recognized the earthly Jesus and His authority. In this passage Paul declared that in like manner the principalities and powers recognize the manifold wisdom of God through the church.

It burdens me when I see persons, who call themselves "Christians," treat the church with disdain. We do so when we allow petty hurts to disrupt our fellowship and affect our ministry. We do so when we are lackadaisical about our commitment in giving, or teaching, or serving. We must fully become what we are called and empowered to be.

We cannot neglect the truth that, by virtue of our faith "in Christ," we are caught up in a divine purpose that spans eternity (v. 11). Just as the redemptive work of the cross was an accomplished fact in the heart of God before the foundation of the earth, so was God's plan for the church. The church is completely bound, throughout eternity, to the redemptive work of Christ, for it is His body. This helps us understand why

the resurrected Lord would question Saul on the road to
Damascus: "Saul, Saul, why are you persecuting Me?" (Acts
9:4) To persecute the church was in truth to persecute Christ,
for the church is His body.

The knowledge of who we are in Christ should give us confidence in prayer. If the One in whom we have access to the
Father is the One in whom the eternal purpose of God is
bound up and we are His body, we can have "boldness" and
confident access through faith in Him.

The Greek word translated "boldness" denotes freedom of
utterance or plainness of speech. In classical Greek the word
would be used to signify the free speech that was the right of
every citizen in a democracy. In the context of the Christian
community, it is the right and privilege of the believer to
approach God confidently through no intermediary other than
Christ. This boldness translated itself into Paul's ministry in
such a manner that he could glory in suffering for the sake of
the gospel.

Too much is at stake for us not to live up to our heritage. For
this reason the apostle Paul was moved again to exercise confident prayer. The intensity of this prayer can be seen in the
phrase "I bow my knees before the Father" (Eph. 3:14). Standing was the usual posture of prayer for the Jews. Kneeling for
prayer was an expression of deep emotion or earnestness. Thus
we must pay close attention to the content of this prayer.

Notice, if you will, that the prayer begins with a highly
personal and individual emphasis "that He would grant you"
(v. 16). Then it shades quickly into the corporate or community
idea: "may be able to comprehend with all the saints" (v. 18).
The point is this: the church will only begin to realize its
potential as its individual members begin to realize and appropriate what is available to them in Christ. We also can flip that
coin and declare the parallel truth. We will individually experience what God has in store for us only in the context of the
body of Christ.

Strength in the Inner Man

Paul's first prayer (1:15-23) was his concern for strength. This
prayer essentially begins where that first prayer left off. If
there is anything that we need to fully realize our potential, it
is strength. How often do we hear people confess, "I'm just

serving the Lord in my poor, weak little way!" The truth of that statement becomes all too apparent as we see the inability of churches to make any significant inroads into our society.

In 1976 in Norfolk, Virginia, churches of my denomination set themselves on a course for a bold thrust into missions. We shared great plans and bold goals that I heartily endorsed. But looking at the recent statistics of this plan shows the sad fact that we have not moved forward in meeting this goal. What is true in our life is equally true in many denominations and in individual churches. The church needs to experience the empowering of God through the strengthening of its component parts.

Supernatural strengthening is experienced in the inner being. The "outer man" refers to the body and all that belongs to it. It is thus destined to pass away. The "inner man," however, is the true self. It is the true being that is being renewed day by day (2 Cor. 4:16). It is the self that delights in the law of God (Rom. 7:22).

The apostle Paul once again used several synonyms to suggest the great wealth of power available to the believer. Lest there be any confusion about the abundant resources, Paul reminded the reader that this power is "according to the riches of His glory" (Eph. 3:16). The language in the Greek here is very precise. The verb translated "to be strengthened with power" speaks of being made strong or capable. Paul was speaking of a power that enables us to stand victoriously in the spiritual battle and to serve the Lord victoriously. This power is available to every Christian through the Holy Spirit. Hear these truths! You can stand victoriously! You can serve the Lord effectively!

God promises to give us an enduring strength. I learned about the quality of this enduring strength in the fourth grade. Our family moved to Thomasville that year, and I had a fourth grade teacher who was very difficult. Report cards in the fourth grade are quite enlightening. Instead of letter grades like A's, B's, and C's, they graded with S's, O's, and U's. On the back of the report card there would be a comment about the pupil. I really dreaded these impromptu ramblings of my teachers. My mom really appreciated comments like, "Does Ken own a clean shirt?" Like most moms she sent me to school in a clean shirt. I just couldn't seem to arrive that way.

On one particular report card I remember getting a comment that was truly exciting. The teacher wrote, "Ken's greatest attribute is his tenaciousness." Now remember, I was in the fourth grade. I couldn't even pronounce it, much less define it. My dilemma was obvious. I didn't know if this was good or bad. But I had a plan. I knew that Dad would be home when I arrived with my report card. I decided to hand him my report card and step back to a safe distance to see whether he smiled or frowned. If he smiled, I would ask for a definition. If he frowned, I would beat a hasty retreat and discuss it when Mom got home. My plan proceeded smoothly except for one small hitch. My dad read the comment without the slightest change of facial expression. I faced a huge dilemma, but my curiosity was at full tilt. I had to risk it! "Dad, what does t-e-n-a-c-i-o-u-s-n-e-s-s mean?" Wisely he looked over his newspaper and responded: "I could tell you, son, but that wouldn't do you any good. You need to look it up!" Now that I'm a parent I realize my dad's response is what parents say when they don't know the answer. He didn't have a clue!

To look up a word one must have a dictionary. Dictionaries are helpful tools for a fourth grader. I finally found "tenaciousness." The definition was illuminating: "the act of being tenacious." Really helpful! OK, let's back up to *tenacious*. The first four or five definitions used words I didn't understand, and I really didn't want to spend the evening using the dictionary. I read down to definition *F* or *G* and found one that I could understand: "Has an attitude like a bulldog." I still wasn't sure if it was good or bad. My dad assured me that the teacher was being positive. She was saying that I was determined. Tenaciousness is the quality that grabs on and does not let go. Like a bulldog, it endures.

We have this tenacious strength in Christ. We can live victoriously. We can serve God effectively. This strength for service enables us to live out our heritage. We so often fail to experience this level of power because we are afraid to push ourselves past our own energies. We want to stick to familiar territory. A nominating committee asks us to serve in a new capacity. We recoil because we've never tried it. We can't do it! We're challenged to dream a new dream for church growth. We're afraid we might fail, so we shrink back. Thus we forfeit opportunities to experience this empowering for service that is a supernatural work of the Holy Spirit.

Experience the Indwelling of Christ (v. 17)

Notice that there is both an obvious and a close connection between the empowering of the Holy Spirit in the inner man and the indwelling of Christ. There is much confusion in our day about the ministry of the Holy Spirit. The empowering of the Spirit and the indwelling of Christ are not two different experiences but one. We are empowered by the Spirit in direct proportion to the union that we have with Christ. The daily infilling with the Spirit comes through our surrender to Christ.

The idea conveyed by "dwell" is to take up residence. Paul's prayer was that Christ would take up residence in their hearts. The location of the heart indicates the very center of our being. Your daughter will use *heart* in this sense when she comes home and announces: "Dad, I love him with all my heart." She doesn't mean a muscle pumping blood, but the essence of her being. Could it be that we miss out on His strength because He is Lord of our tongues and not of our hearts? We talk about discipleship, and we sing songs pledging our allegiance. We discuss what could be if we ever truly surrendered. We meet in our mission groups and Sunday School classes and talk about the profound implications of the church. We even talk about the way discipleship could be done. Yet it rarely gets done.

I had the privilege of playing football at Wake Forest University. I was recruited with an outstanding freshman class in 1966. During my era, freshmen were not allowed to play varsity ball. Our freshman team had a great season, going 6-0 for the year. We were looking forward to our sophomore season with new uniforms and possibly a new stadium. We were scheduled to move from the old Bowman Gray Stadium to a new facility across town at Groves Stadium. The stadium was not prepared in time, but we started the season with great enthusiasm. Our new old-gold helmets with modern logos, crisp gold pants, and gleaming white jerseys with gold-on-black numerals looked great.

There was a minor hitch. We weren't playing up to expectations. I remember one particular game where the score grew more lopsided as the game progressed. Nothing was going right, and the enthusiasm of the fans began to wane by half time. The stands grew more vacant and the crowd more silent as the time wore on. That is to say, with the exception of my dad. Now you need to know that my dad is the eternal optimist. He can see the silver lining behind every cloud. He is an encourager. As the stands emptied, he kept improving his seat. Finally, he was down front on the fifty-yard line. He was still yelling as if the outcome were still in question.

As the seconds ticked down, I began to watch my dad. I knew exactly what he was going to do. When the horn sounded, he would jump the wall, run down on the field, and congratulate me with some positive comment on our performance. This last part of the formula bothered me most. We were getting slaughtered. What would he possibly find good to say about this performance? I had decided that if he said anything good about the game, I would deck him right there on the field. Now bear in mind if I had hit my father it would have been my only tackle of the day, and I played linebacker on defense.

The horn sounded! I sprinted for the clubhouse hoping to get inside before my dad could find me. No luck! He beat me there! He should have been playing, not me. He came up, threw his arm around me, and declared: "You guys looked great!" *Looked great*, I thought. *Which game had he been watching? Maybe the sun had gotten to him.* But after a short pause he finished his statement, "In the huddle." He was right, we did look good in the huddle. We had crisp new uniforms, and mine for once wasn't even dirty. We lined up in good order. We broke the huddle crisply, and we hustled to the line of scrimmage. We really did look good in the huddle. Our trouble started when we snapped the ball.

That's our problem in the church. We get into our mission groups and talk strategy for winning the world. We dream about the potential of our evangelistic programs, and we can call the right plays. But we seem to be having trouble getting off the line of scrimmage. We gather in our Sunday School classes and talk about the power of God's Word to change lives, but we watch helplessly as divorce destroys the roll of our own class. We sit in our deacons' meeting and talk about what we could do if we ever made our budget; then we dismiss and limp back to the line of scrimmage, not expecting anything to change. We must turn rhetoric into reality and promise into practice.

To turn our talk into reality requires faith. God's power is unleashed "through faith." Christ waits for us to be willing for Him to come in with the fullness of His blessing. We must believe and abandon ourselves to Him. We must move expectantly at His command, trusting that He is sufficient to supply all our needs according to the riches of His glory.

Know the Love of Christ

Paul's goal was that they would come to know the love of Christ. An obvious paradox is present in the text: Paul prayed that they would *know* a love that by definition "surpasses *knowledge*" (author's italics). The love of Christ is beyond human comprehension. We are not to give carefully prescribed meanings to words like *length* and *height* and *depth* as they describe the love of Christ. These words are to be experienced with the heart as we confront the many dimensions of Christ's love available to the believer.

This experiential knowledge of the love of Christ is the very foundation of the Christian community. Paul used two different word pictures to communicate this truth. The word *grounded* pictures the foundation of a building that provides a stable platform for building. *Rooted* pictures a tree with a root system that deeply penetrates the soil providing both nurture and stability. The experience of Christ's love is that which provides the stability and sustenance for church growth.

We must not neglect the truth that the knowledge of the love of Christ is not attainable in isolation, but it is experienced "with all the saints." It is in the context of the Christian family with all of its ragged edges, bumps, and bruises that we come to know the love of Christ.

The paradox of knowing that which surpasses knowing is solved by due attention to the present context. In the body, I can know through experience one facet of God's love while you might know another and so on throughout the congregation. For example, I know of one rich dimension of God's love through my joyous experience of loving parents. Perhaps you cannot know that. You may, however, know of a different facet of God's love who has walked with you through a painful divorce or a tragic death. I have never experienced those. But my knowledge of God's love grows as I learn of this different dimension of His love from you. Now when we bring the entire body together we can literally know God's love which surpasses knowing for any one believer.

I feel sorry for people who want to pretend that they are so spiritual that they can't find a church deep enough or pure enough for them. I am equally concerned with supposed Christians who believe they can get along quite well without the fellowship of the church. Certainly, there are those times of conflict in the church when we all feel we could manage the Christian life OK if it wasn't for all the Christians we have to put up with. However, we are family! And it is in the context of God's family that we learn to experience and express the love of Christ. Remember the words of our Lord, "Truly I say to you, to the extent that you did it to one of these brothers of Mine, even the least of them, you did it to Me" (Matt. 25:40).

The very stability of our existence is discovered in the experience of Christ's love in community. Our growth in the knowledge of Christ's love is essential to the church realizing its potential.

Filled with the Fulness of God

Paul concluded His prayer with the request that we "be filled up to all the fulness of God" (v. 19). You will recall that in our last chapter we commented on a similar phrase in Ephesians 1:23. In that section Paul prayed that the Ephesians might come to understand that the church was "the fulness of Him who fills all in all." Now Paul took his request a step further and prayed that the readers might individually and collectively be filled to the "fulness of God." The point is this: the church will only become what it is destined to be—"the fulness of Him who fills all in all"—when we become individually what we are called to be. This is not a specific gift or attribute, but it is everything we need to be made complete: the full indwelling of God Himself.

The theme of fullness plays a great role in Ephesians and its twin letter, Colossians. Apparently there was great interest and speculation concerning the experience of the "fulness" (*pleroma*). Paul affirmed in Colossians 2:9 that in Christ "the fulness of Deity dwells in bodily form." Therefore, it is in Christ that the individual believer has been made complete (2:10). This same truth is applied both to the church and to the individual in Ephesus. If the fulness is in Christ, it is expressed and experienced through the church by virtue of the fact that the church is the body of Christ.

Those who want to believe they can experience the fullness of Christ outside the context of the church must give due attention to the theme of Ephesians. Christ expresses His fullness in His body. We need nothing else to be made complete: no New Age enlightenment, no second blessings, or a baptism of the Spirit subsequent to salvation. We are made complete in Christ. We must fully appropriate His empowering through the Spirit and set as the constant goal for our churches to grow to maturity, "to the measure of the stature which belongs to the fulness of Christ" (Eph. 4:13).

The great commentator J. Armitage Robinson wrote concerning this prayer: "No prayer that has been framed has uttered a bolder request."[1] Yet Paul unswervingly invoked a God who can do more than we dare ask. It was not that Paul had asked too much. No indeed, for God "is able to do exceeding abundantly beyond all that we ask or think" (Eph. 3:20). This is the power that works within us to bring glory to God in the church and in Christ Jesus. This was not to be a first-century empowering that ended with the death of the apostles. This was "to all generations" (3:21).

Our Father desires to do more than we dream or ask. Paul coined the phrase "exceeding abundantly." We call this phrase a super-superlative. Why do we sell ourselves so short? Why do we behave as if the church today is impotent? God desires to bring glory to Himself, to demonstrate to the world His manifold wisdom (3:10).

My early ministry at First Baptist, Norfolk, was blessed with great results. We were privileged to see people walk the aisles weekly. Soon the church outgrew my ability. My Sunday School director, Dick Baker, and I headed off to a denominationally sponsored growth conference. I learned a great deal about setting goals for quality Sunday School growth.

On the drive home, Dick and I discussed the conference. We decided that the first step we should take was to help our church have a great dream for Sunday School growth. We decided that we would call all the Sunday School leaders in, share what we had learned, and challenge them to set goals. In a few weeks, Dick came back to me and announced that our enrollment goal for that year was 840, an increase of nearly 68 percent over our present enrollment of 1200 pushing our enrollment to 2,040. I didn't know that the goal was impossible for a church our size, so I nodded my approval. The goal was announced, banners were placed throughout the church, and our new Sunday School year was off to a running start.

In the ensuing weeks, I was thumbing through the various church newsletters I receive. I began to notice that the other churches our size were announcing goals of 8 percent or 12 percent but not 68 percent. I called Dick into my office and showed him those papers. "What do you mean by such an outrageous goal?" I asked him.

He responded, "You said to dream a great dream, didn't you?"

"Don't you hate it when people remind you of your preaching?" *Great dreams are one thing*, I thought, *but this is crazy!*

Calmly he responded, "I think we can do it. All the teachers believe we can do it. Let's give it a try."

We left the banners up and kept the goal. When the end of the year rolled around, we discovered that we had actually exceeded our goal.

What caused such a surge in Sunday School growth? Excellence of pastoral leadership? Hardly! I was still wet behind the ears, barely able to find the pulpit. The church dared to dream a great dream. The vision ignited the spark that caused us to pray and work together. Through us, God accomplished the impossible. God is able to do beyond that which we dream or ask. He does so "according to the power that works within us" (v. 20).

A church living out its heritage gives glory to God, both in the church and in Christ Jesus. Move on from check to checkmate; experience what God intends for your church to be. Your church can grow. It can reach your community! We simply cannot afford to play at church. To waste God's great power on insignificant goals would be a great tragedy. We must live our heritage. Dare to dream a great dream for God. Be the church!

Notes

1. J. Armitage Robinson, *Commentary on Ephesians* (Michigan: Kregel Publications, 1979), 89.

5

Playing House

For He Himself is our peace, who made both groups into one, and broke down the barrier of the dividing wall, by abolishing in His flesh the enmity, which is the Law of commandments contained in ordinances, that in Himself He might make the two into one new man, thus establishing peace, and might reconcile them both in one body to God through the cross, by it having put to death the enmity.

So then you are no longer strangers and aliens, but you are fellow citizens with the saints, and are of God's household, having been built upon the foundation of the apostles and prophets, Christ Jesus Himself being the corner stone, in whom the whole building, being fitted together is growing into a holy temple in the Lord; in whom you also are being built together into a dwelling of God in the Spirit.

—Ephesians 2:14-16, 19-22

Playing house was not among my top ten favorite games. I really didn't like it at all, but somehow it was one of those early childhood duties. I often wondered why girls got such a kick out of playing house. Who could possibly want to pretend cooking or pretend going shopping? *Yucky* was my only word to describe it.

Now as a parent, I have been amused to watch my own children play house. Most of the time my girls and their little girlfriends have played house with their dolls. It's cute to watch as a parent. Things appear to go pretty smoothly in the pretend households. Barbie drives a shiny red sports car, and Ken is the all-American guy. They have nice clothes, plenty of fun accessories, and lots of friends. Their friends have to be purchased, of course.

Yet things seldom seem to go so smoothly in real life. We don't all look like Ken and Barbie, and marriages don't always go smoothly. For many people, friends are not found in abundance. Many people today feel left out, excluded. Real life is nothing like playing house.

Words like loneliness, isolation, and alienation occur frequently in print today. We have become a transient nation, and many folks feel like a number in the crowd. The people surrounding them are faceless and anonymous acquaintances. Even in childhood we fear being left alone. A child awakens only to discover that he or she is alone in the house. Mom may only be in the front yard talking to a neighbor, but for an instant there is that awful feeling of panic, desperation, and loneliness. But I think a more frightening experience of childhood is finding yourself alone in a crowd. Did you ever become separated from your parents at a ball game or in a shopping center? You may have paused a moment to look at that new bike in a store window, and when you turned around, you were alone. There may have been hundreds of people nearby, but no one that you recognized. The presence of all those "strangers" actually heightened your sense of being alone. *Is there no one here that I know?*

Many folks in our neighborhoods, our offices, our schools, and in our churches feel isolated and alone in the crowd. After preaching a sermon on this text in Norfolk, a young lady came to see me. She began by telling me that she was one of those folks who was isolated in the crowd. She wanted to break out, to know, and to be known; but she was paralyzed by the very idea. She had a twofold fear. She was afraid that someone in her Sunday School class might actually speak to her, and she would have to respond. But paradoxically, she was afraid no one would speak to her. Thus she often arrived after the class had started to avoid confronting her own fears, and she remained alone.

How do we as a church family provide a dimension of fellowship that reaches to those who are alone in the crowd? How can we create a church family that is not make-believe? How do we involve those who argue that they don't want or need fellowship? No matter what we say, we are created for fellowship. On the opening pages of Scripture we confront the unquestionable truth, "It is not good for the man to be alone" (Gen. 2:18). While this verse deals with marriage companionship, it also points up a person's basic need for fellowship. We should not be surprised that the world provides numerous counterfeits designed to meet this basic need of humankind. Clubs, fraternities, organizations, and societies of all types abound. Bruce Larson called the neighborhood bar the greatest counterfeiter of fellowship in our day.

> It is an imitation, dispensing liquor instead of grace, escape rather than reality, but it is a permissive, accepting and inclusive fellowship. . . . The bar flourishes not because most people are alcoholics, but because God has put into the human heart the desire to know and to be known, to love and be loved.[1]

In a recent report, given at the World Congress on Evangelism, George Gallup concluded that there is a renewed search today for more meaningful relationships. People are discovering the futility of going it alone.[2] They are seeking more than surface relationships provided by clubs, fraternities, bars, and the like. The church has a wonderful opportunity to meet this need.

Introductory Concerns

The matter of Christian fellowship is so vital to the life of the Christian church that we must give it close attention. Following are a few fundamental principles that must be recognized.

1. *Fellowship is not an option in biblical Christianity.*—We need only think about Jesus' final instructions to His disciples as recorded in the Gospel of John to see the absolute necessity of fellowship. In His final instructions Jesus repeated a singular command three times (John 13:34; 15:12,17). "A new commandment I give to you, that you love one another, even as I have loved you, that you also love one another" (John 13:34). The context of this command was the sharing of the Passover meal. In the course of the evening, Jesus demonstrated love by washing the feet of His disciples. He told the disciples that people would recognize them as His followers "if you have love for one another" (John 13:35). It is an inescapable truth that you cannot belong to Christ without belonging to and loving your brothers and sisters in Christ.

2. *Fellowship with other believers is essential to personal spiritual growth.*—In Ephesians 3:18-19 we confronted the curious but profound truth that it is together "with all the saints" that we "know the love of Christ." To think that we will

grow in our spiritual walk while neglecting fellowship in the body of Christ is utter folly.

3. *Fellowship is essential to the work of the church because it is the basis for the functioning of the gifted body.*—We will look at the ministry of gifts in chapter 11. Suffice it to say, at this point, that the unity of Christian fellowship is an absolute necessity for the proper working of the body.

4. *Authentic fellowship can only be found in Christ.*—One of the key words for describing fellowship in the New Testament is *koinonia* from the root *koinos* or "common, mutual, or public." Uses of *koinonia* in secular Greek in the time of the New Testament were numerous. For example, a neighborhood might have a public park. The park was *koinos* because it belonged to everyone. When applied to people, *koinonia* could refer to a business partnership or a marriage partnership. For example, two people entered into marriage to have a *koinonia* of life. It could also be used in the Greek and Hellenistic world to point to the relationship between the gods and people. While *koinonia* is absent from the Gospels, it is common to the Pauline Letters. Paul never used *koinonia* in any of these secular senses. For Paul, *koinonia* was not an earthly society grounded in common interests, but a community grounded in the common experience of Christ. Paul spoke of Christians being called into fellowship with Jesus Christ, our Lord (1 Cor. 1:9). He desired for them the fellowship of the Holy Spirit (2 Cor. 13:14). The right hand of fellowship (Gal. 2:9) was not a handshake to welcome new members, but a recognition of mutual authority and relationship because of one's position in Christ.[3] Having looked at these fundamental principles, we must now look at the foundation for biblical fellowship.

Salvation: The Prerequisite

The first section of Ephesians 2 contains the profound message of personal redemption. Our condition outside of Christ is described with terms like "dead in your trespasses and sins" (v. 1) and "children of wrath" (v. 3). But because God's rich mercy flowed out of His great love for us, He has made us alive together with Christ (v. 5). His desire is to show His children "the surpassing riches of His grace in kindness toward us in Christ" (v. 7). While these are overwhelming personal truths, you should not fail to note that the context already hints at our corporate experience in Christ. He has "raised us" and "seated us" in order to show us His riches. God's purpose in our redemption is to build a community in which He can demonstrate to the whole creation the magnitude of His mercy, grace, and love: "For we are His workmanship" (v. 10).

We enjoy displaying our workmanship. My children are creative. In the early years it was not always obvious what they had created. At times I was forced to look at a drawing from several different vantage points as I turned the sheet from corner to corner hoping for revelation. Dancing eyes and eager ears awaited my pronouncement, "This is a beautiful house." We simply enjoy creating and then showing others our creation so that they may share our joy. Paul told us that God Himself enjoys displaying the church, His workmanship, to the world. Can you hear God saying as He holds the church up before all the spiritual powers: "Look, this is what I do; this is my creation."

Paul now looked at these salvation truths from the context of his own ministry to the Gentiles. Paul reminded his readers that they were once "excluded from the commonwealth of Israel, and strangers to the covenants of promise, having no hope and without God in the world" (v. 12). This was because they were "separate from Christ." This phrase is the basic description of the dilemma of the Gentiles. All the other descriptions given in the text are based on the one essential truth that they were "spearate from Christ." Did you hear those words of isolation? Aliens! Strangers! Excluded! No hope! All of these come from humanity's essential separation from God.

But now in Christ the inconceivable has happened. The Gentiles have been brought near to God by the sacrifice of Jesus Christ. The prerequisite for fellowship with any person or group of persons is the establishment of fellowship with God. There is no true *koinōnia* outside of Jesus Christ. This is why all other attempts at fellowship are partial at best and counterfeit and misleading at worst. Notice that fellowship is first of all a "state or condition" determined by one's relationship to God. Only as we have fellowship with God through Christ are we prepared to engage in specific acts of fellowship with other believers.

In college I felt I had to join a fraternity. After all, "everybody else" was joining a fraternity. I didn't want to be left out. I wanted to belong. Against the advice of several friends, I went ahead with my plans. Each evening we pledges were assigned various tasks to prove our worthiness. One evening we were given a really easy assignment. Write a short paper on brotherhood. Simple enough! I could dash that off in minutes and have plenty of time for a little television. All my pledge brothers finished the assignment quickly, but I was stuck. No matter how hard I tried, I could not write this short paper on brotherhood. I thought about brotherhood and fellowship in the context of the Bible. I knew that many of my future "brothers" were non-Christians. I did not have much in common with many of these men. They were good guys, but they weren't and never could be my brothers in the full sense of that word. I would write a few sentences and rip that page off and start again. I finally completed my task, but I knew my paper lacked integrity. I have never forgotten that exercise. I have remained friends with some of those men, and I am delighted to say that several of them are indeed my brothers. But authentic brotherhood and fellowship are only found in Christ.

Fellow Citizens with the Saints

Absolutely no class distinction, racial division, or cultural separation exists today that is any more pronounced than was the wall of separation between the Jew and the Gentile in the days of the New Testament church. The Jews looked upon the Gentiles as "dogs," and that was one of their polite names for them. Nothing could bridge this gap. There was no way, humanly speaking, that these two groups of people would ever come together!

Yet Christ made both groups into one. Paul underlined this truth with numerous word pictures. He has broken down "the dividing wall" (v. 14), He has made "the two into one new man" (v. 15), He has reconciled "them both in one body" (v. 16), and He has "put to death the enmity" (v. 16). The sins of the Jews and Gentiles alike were abolished by Christ's death on the cross (v. 16).

When persons are brought near to God through Christ and continue to abide in Him, they find peace with one another. Divisions are not solved by compromise on either side but by peace in Christ. "The way of salvation" is singular, and, there-fore, Jew and Gentile must all come together at this point of access to God through the cross. The peace that comes through response to the proclamation of the gospel puts us all on common footing in the presence of God the Father.

Paul was particularly concerned about the practical dividing wall between the strict Jews and Gentiles. The age-old enmity was real, and feelings of hostility don't die easily. The dividing wall that was hardest to scale was "the Law of commandments contained in ordinances" (v. 15). This phrase refers to the Law with its detailed ordinances concerning the ceremonies and regulations about the clean and unclean. It was these external ordinances, guiding the details of daily living, that made the Jew distinct from the Gentile. Jesus came to fulfill the moral demands and principles of the Law, but His coming did away with ordinances such as circumcision and food preparation that had proved so divisive. Thus, when the Jew and the Gentile came to God through Christ, these external differences were dealt a death blow. Yet we must put into practice the realities that our redemption makes possible. We must not allow these walls of division to be reconstructed in our church fellowships.

Today traditions still can be divisive. Disagreement on matters such as dancing, movies, mixed swimming, and appropriate activities for Sunday afternoons can still destroy fellowship. While some of these things involve moral issues that cannot themselves be ignored, we cannot allow our fellowship to be destroyed by dependence on tradition or slavery to legalistic codes. Our common experience of Christ is still that which enables us to share fellowship despite such differences.

Paul used three pictures to express the unity that emerges from our redemption. The term "fellow citizens" calls to mind one's citizenship which is the sense of belonging and having the legal rights that go with citizenship. The Gentiles, there-fore, are "no longer strangers and aliens." "God's household" is a more intimate picture of a family unit (v. 19). When we are born into Christ, we are born into a family where relationships with others is a necessity. The final picture is in the word "building." We are part of a divine building being constructed by God Himself, and thus our integral relationship with one another is essential to the growth and stability of the building.

You will not experience genuine church growth on a long-term basis unless the church develops a deep sense of biblical fellowship.

The Sevenfold Basis of Fellowship

In Ephesians 4 Paul entreated the believers to walk in a manner worthy of their calling. One aspect of our worthy walk is our diligence in preserving "the unity of the Spirit in the bond of peace" (v. 3). This exhortation is followed by a reminder of the sevenfold unity we have in Christ Jesus. "There is one body and one Spirit, just as also you were called in one hope of your calling; one Lord, one faith, one baptism, one God and Father of all who is over all and through all and in all" (4:4-6). Let's look at those things we have in common. These form the true basis of our *koinōnia*.

1. *One body.*—Here Paul referred to the church, the body of Christ, that is made up of all believers. We who are many are actually *one* body in Christ.

2. *One Spirit.*—The Holy Spirit is in view here. It is He alone who gives life and unity to the church, even as He inaugurated it on the day of Pentecost.

3. *One hope of your calling.*—You will recall our discussion of our calling in Ephesians 1:18. We are thus to remember that we all share the same high calling to experience His riches and His glory.

4. *One Lord.*—Our one Lord is Jesus Christ Himself. In Romans 14 Paul appealed to the lordship of Christ to bring unity to the Roman Christians. They were divided over dietary and worship considerations. Paul declared that while some regarded one day and some another, we all observe it for the Lord. Then he asked, "Why do you regard your brother with contempt? For we shall all stand before the judgment seat of God" (Rom. 14:10). Our brotherhood has its origin in our common relationship to "one Lord."

5. *One faith.*—Commentators debate whether faith means the act of believing or the substance of one's belief. It is not either/or, but both/and. Our belief in the historical Christ as our Lord is that which gives substance to faith and unity to the church. We share one faith.

6. *One baptism.*—The outward and visible sign of the church's one faith was baptism. Much conflict has been created

in the modern-day church by the suggestion that there are two baptisms, one in water and one in the Spirit. Some of those who call themselves charismatics or Pentecostals suggest that a Christian must experience a Spirit baptism subsequent to water baptism. But as F. F. Bruce pointed out, "When water baptism and Spirit baptism are set in opposition in the New Testament, the water baptism is John's baptism and not Christian baptism."[4] The point is that the New Testament does not teach a second baptism in the Spirit after the act of Christian water baptism. When the Spirit descended upon the first Gentile believers, Peter commanded them "to be baptized in the name of Jesus Christ" (Acts 10:48). Baptism in water was the outward, visible sign that individuals who had repented of their sins and acknowledged Jesus as Lord were incorporated into this Spirit-empowered community. The baptism in the Spirit occurs at salvation and is signified by our water baptism. Even in the conflict-torn Corinthian community where persons claimed to be spirituals, based on the possession of certain spiritual gifts, Paul declared, "For by one Spirit we were all baptized into one body, whether Jews or Greeks, whether slaves or free, and we were all made to drink of one Spirit" (1 Cor. 12:13). There is one baptism! This *one baptism* is a source of unity: "For all of you who were baptized into Christ have clothed yourselves with Christ. There is neither Jew nor Greek, there is neither slave nor free man, there is neither male nor female; for you are all one in Christ Jesus" (Gal. 3:27-28).

7. *One God and Father.*—We are all God's by creation, and all believers are His children by redemption in Christ. We are of necessity related to one another because we all have one Father.

We will not create fellowship by simply setting aside a room in our church for activities that usually center around eating. We will not create it simply by the formation of small groups. Fellowship is first of all a common experience of faith—a unique and divine work of the Holy Spirit. It comes from a true grasp of who we are in Christ. We must teach this sevenfold unity as the basis for fellowship.

Built Together

Salvation, while it must be received personally and individually, is never an isolated experience. By our incorporation in Christ we become part of the building He is constantly constructing. Jesus promised His disciples that *He* would build His church (Matt. 16:18).

Looking back at Ephesians 2:20-22, we discover the third picture of Christ in fellowship—that of a building. The believers who received this letter were not the first stones in the temple, but they were built upon stones already in place. The foundation stones were the apostles and prophets of the first century, the Lord's foundational gifts to the church (see 1 Cor. 12:28). Christ is pictured as the chief cornerstone. The cornerstone was cut out before hand. When it was dropped into place it formed a bond that welded the structure together and assured that it had been built according to the architect's specifications.

You might recall that in 1 Corinthians 3:11 Paul depicted Christ as the foundation of the building. In our present context Paul pictured Christ's relation to the building with another image—that of the chief cornerstone. These two ideas are not contradicting, they simply emphasize different theological truths. In 1 Corinthians Paul focused on the work of the builders of the temple, himself being a wise master builder. He asserted that all builders must be careful to build on the one true foundation. In Ephesians all believers are pictured as stones in a building which is itself growing. The image is similar to that of 1 Peter 2:4-10. Jesus is presented as the cornerstone because of the focus on His function of binding the building together. Christ was the source of peace for Jews and Gentiles; He was the one way of access to the Father. He is our source of unity, binding us all together.

Notice too that we are "fitted together" and "being built together." God's purpose in the church is to make it His dwelling place on earth. Christ, as cornerstone, not only binds all the stones together; but He becomes the source of its fellowship and its growth. Paul actually used a biological verb, "growing," to speak of the church as a building. The church is a living organism, empowered by the living Christ to grow. Church growth should be natural for the New Testament community.

The verb translated "being fitted together" is found in the New Testament only here and in Ephesians 4:16. While it is true that it is the sovereign empowering of God that enables the church to grow, it is nonetheless important that each individual member participate in that growth. Notice in Ephesians 4:16 that the imagery is that of the physical body which grows through the proper working of each individual part. Yet, even in that context, it is the head, Christ, who causes the growth of the body. Fellowship is the foundation for the proper operation of the gifts.

Fellowship is essential to church growth and the foundation for our individual growth. All too frequently I hear the suggestion that we must sacrifice fellowship if we desire church growth. Nothing could be further from the truth. Fellowship and church growth are partners. In Christ we are "being built together into a dwelling of God in the Spirit" (v. 22). God made His presence known in the tabernacle and the Temple in the Old Testament days. He then fully indwelt His Son during the days of His incarnation. Now with the resurrection and ascension of His Son, God's presence and power are discovered in His people—His church—where God has chosen to make His dwelling place on earth. We cannot escape the implications of these great biblical truths. We must be diligent to maintain the unity created by the Holy Spirit in order that we might fully reveal His presence.

Notes

1. Bruce Larson, *Dare to Love Now* (Grand Rapids: Zondervan, 1965), 110.

2. George Gallup, "Worldwide Trends in Religion" (Speech given at the Biennial Meeting of the lausanne Committee for World Evangelization, Atlanta, 22 January 1987), 22.

3. Johannes Schattenmann, *"koinonia,"* in *The New International Dictionary of New Testament Theology*, 4 vols. (Grand Rapids: Zondervan Publishing House, Regency Reference Library, 1986), 1:639-644.

4. F. F. Bruce, *The Epistle to the Ephesians* (London: Pickering Inglis Ltd., 1961), 78-79.

6

Let's Play Blocks

What was from the beginning, what we have heard, what we have seen with our eyes, what we beheld and our hands handled, concerning the Word of Life—and the life was manifested, and we have seen and bear witness and proclaim to you the eternal life, which was with the Father and was manifested to us—what we have seen and heard we proclaim to you also, that you also may have fellowship with us; and indeed our fellowship is with the Father, and with His Son Jesus Christ. And these things we write, so that our joy may be made complete.

If we say that we have fellowship with Him and yet walk in the darkness, we lie and do not practice the truth; but if we walk in the light as He Himself is in the light, we have fellowship with one another, and the blood of Jesus His Son cleanses us from all sin.

—1 John 1:1-4, 6-7

Let's play blocks! One of the games that children learn to play first is one of the simplest and most fundamental of all games: blocks. The blocks that I still remember were simple wooden shapes lacking stain or finish of any sort. They were relatively inexpensive, possibly homemade, yet they fascinated me for hours. It's interesting how the simpler and more basic games are often the most popular. I first enjoyed seeing how high I could stack my blocks before they would fall. As I got older the shapes of the blocks became fascinating, and I began to design forts and castles with them. Blocks have a certain fascination that keep drawing children back at various ages of childhood development. I confess I still have trouble passing them up in the church preschool. The only frustration with playing blocks is that there is frequently someone who insists on knocking them down. In my case it was an older brother. This would bring the usual flow of tears, then I would start building again.

We have more sophisticated blocks today such as Lincoln Logs, Legos, bristle blocks, etc., but their function is basically the same. I am told that playing blocks improves hand-eye coordination and encourages creativity. Actually it is a great teaching game. I certainly didn't play blocks for that reason, but I'm sure I must have benefited.

If blocks is one of the most basic of games, then fellowship would be its parallel in the church. Research reveals that a majority of people attend a particular church because of the quality of its fellowship. In fact, a whopping 79 percent of persons surveyed indicated that they attended a certain church because they were invited by a friend or relative. The implication should be obvious. These people are looking for fellowship. They come to church because they sense someone cares. Fellowship, like blocks, costs little in terms of program dollars, but it yields rich dividends in the continuing development of the church. As programs in our church wax and wane, our personal relationships keep us coming back. If we could improve the quality of the fellowship in our churches, we would begin to see them grow in a dramatic way.

The greatest need of our day is fellowship, real biblical caring that goes deeper than surface friendships. All around our churches are masses of hurting folks: people whose self-esteem has been wounded by the loss of employment, families reeling from the impact of children in rebellion, and persons struggling with an addiction to drugs or alcohol. Others are grieving due to a loss caused by death or divorce. People are longing for companionship. They desperately are seeking someone to share their sorrows and their joys, someone who will listen and perhaps pray with them.

Fellowship must become a priority issue of the church. No one else can provide this community where real *koinōnia* is experienced. Only the New Testament church has the possibility to develop this deep level of fellowship. Yet it is frequently not experienced in many of our churches today. Too much is at stake to leave this to chance. We must therefore give careful attention to the building blocks for fellowship.

Proclamation: The Pathway to Fellowship (vv. 1-3)

Proclamation literally explodes from the first three verses of
1 John 1. Notice that John declared his desire was to "bear
witness" and *"proclaim"* the eternal life. In verse 3, John
joined other witnesses in declaring that which they had seen
and heard so others would share their fellowship. Thus we
should first notice that the pathway to true biblical fellowship
is proclamation of the gospel.

The opening words of this chapter remind us of the opening
words of the Gospel of John. We are hurtled back into the
infinite past of eternity. From the beginning of time the "Word
of Life" (1 John 1:1) was with the Father. Yet John's emphasis
here was not on eternity past but on the manifestation of the
"Word of Life" in the flesh. The stacking up of verbs related
to the senses—"heard," "seen," "beheld," and "handled"—
focus on the incarnation as a historical event that demands
both declaration and response. The "Word of Life" became
flesh, so much so that He could be seen, heard, and touched.
Possibly the phrase "our hands handled" (v. 1) may echo the
challenge of the risen Jesus to the doubting disciples in Luke
24:39, "Touch Me and see." Whether this is the case or not, the
phrase "our hands handled" is an intensely personal testimony
of the early apostles' personal experience of the "Word of
Life."

The One who became flesh and thus was manifested in historical time and space was the very "Word of Life." Scholars
vary concerning John's use of the word *logos* (Word). Certainly
there is a clear connection with the Old Testament where the
Word of the Lord was the powerful activity of God in creation
and revelation (Gen. 1:3; Pss. 33:6; 107:20; 147:15). The Stoics
(Greek philosophers) frequently used *logos* as the "principle of
reason" giving meaning to the universe. It is conceivable that
logos was a part of the intellectual discussion of John's day. In
that case, John may have used this term to catch the reader's
attention. Alexander Ross paraphrased this verse as follows:
"Here is what you have been vainly fumbling after in your
philosophical speculations, here is the solution of the "riddle of
the universe."[1] Whether John's source was that of the Old
Testament or a challenge to the philosophical speculation of
his day, John declared with clear voice: the "Word of Life" has

been manifested in the flesh in Jesus of Nazareth. We can certainly declare this same truth today in a world fumbling to find meaning and purpose.

What thrilling implications this has for church fellowship. Christian fellowship extends from eternity past to eternity future. Yet it has its roots firmly planted in the history of the incarnation. No other organization offers this level or dimension of fellowship. We are indeed "God's forever family" and the "gates of Hades" (Matt. 16:18) cannot overcome this fellowship.

The three verbs in 1 John 1:2 (seen, bear witness, and proclaim) express the ideas of experience, attestation, and evangelism. These ideas form part of a genuine response to the gospel.[2] When we experience the truth of eternal life, we must of necessity bear witness to its reality in our life. This act of testifying may provide us with the opportunity for evangelism.

We must recognize that Christians alone have the privilege to bear witness to eternal life. Eternal life is not simply a reference to the length of life, but to the quality of life. Eternal life is that which the believer shares with the Father and with the Son. It is in Christ, and, therefore, it is abundant life.

John declared that our purpose in declaring the great truth of the incarnation was that "you also may have fellowship with us." This new generation of readers, who have not seen or heard Jesus in the flesh, can now experience fellowship because. of the witness of the first generation of believers. Thus, the way to create and promote fellowship is to proclaim Christ.

It is interesting today that our idea of fellowship is often introverted and thus unbiblical. I frequently hear persons whose church does not emphasize evangelism reply, "We stress fellowship, not evangelism." We can't separate fellowship and evangelism. We declare the gospel in order that fellowship can be extended. So often today we want coziness rather than biblical fellowship. You can hear it in statements like "I'm afraid we may be getting too large to have fellowship." We may get too large to be cozy and keep our cliques in tact. Yes, it is true that when churches reach people for Christ, they will have to start new Sunday School classes or small groups. This may well be inconvenient, but fellowship— biblical fellowship—is experienced and extended through proclamation.

Most people would agree that the church described in the Book of Acts had a deep level of fellowship. The description of this early church in Acts 2:41-47 is replete with phrases indicating deep meaningful relationships. We are told that they were "devoting themselves to the apostles' teaching and to fellowship" (v. 42). Further, we discover that their fellowship was intensely practical as they were selling their property to share with those who had need. They spent time together, "taking their meals together with gladness and sincerity of heart" (v. 46). We would all love to experience a fellowship of this depth. May I call your attention to verses 41 and 47, which literally frame this passage in Acts. This church began with a baptismal service that included about 3,000 persons and continued to grow as "the Lord was adding to their number day by day those who were being saved." We're told in Acts 5:14: "All the more believers in the Lord, multitudes of men and women, were constantly added to their number."

We must forever ban the unbiblical presumption that growth is a threat to our fellowship. Real fellowship can never be diluted by growth. Our selfishness or our unwillingness to change can threaten it but not numerical growth. When we become introverted, when we draw in, we actually forfeit the opportunity for meaningful biblical *koinōnia*.

I know that many of you struggle with this idea of growth and evangelism. I can identify with that struggle. When I was just entering the ministry, I gave the Lord three conditions for my service. It's pretty foolish to think we can negotiate with the Lord of the universe. I was young! I had my mind made up that I didn't want to pastor a First Baptist Church, a church with more than 500 in attendance, or a church that needed to construct buildings.

I have discovered that the Lord often exercises a great sense of humor as He corrects foolish young pastors. Upon returning from England, I was teaching at Wingate College for a year as a visiting professor. During one semester I taught an evening class that was made up primarily of adults from the surrounding community. The class met only one night a week and lasted for about three hours. On this particular evening, we were studying the Book of Acts. During the break, several of the students had gathered around my desk to talk. They inquired about my plans, and I shared with them my desire to pastor a church. I was careful to specify that it should not have more than 500 active members. One of the students replied: "Why Dr. Hemphill, you wouldn't have qualified to pastor the early church in the Book of Acts." How dare he talk to his professor with such insolence! He was right. I had established this mythical number for fellowship. In truth I was limiting God. That was lesson number one.

That same spring I began to talk with a pulpit committee from Galax, Virginia. The interview process went smoothly, and I made a visit to the church field. It was obvious that we were coming down to decision time. The chairman of the pulpit committee called me to talk about coming as their pastor. Truthfully, I had fallen in love with the people and wanted to go, but it was a *First* Baptist Church.

Over the telephone I confessed to the chairman that I had only one reservation: "I just don't like First Baptist churches."

"That's OK," he responded without even a moment's hesitation. "We're even because we don't like preachers with long hair and sideburns."

"That's the silliest thing I ever heard," I retorted.

"I told you we were even."

His homespun wisdom taught me lesson number two. I had to overcome my silly prejudices.

My third lesson came early in my pastorate in Galax. The church plant in Galax is one of the finest facilities in all of Virginia. Yet the plant itself posed one of our greatest problems. It was very large for the size of the community. The church family had outgrown their facilities on Main Street and needed to relocate. With great vision they moved out of town and purchased fourteen beautiful acres. While they were formulating the plans for the new facility the community began gearing up for an influx of new people. The New River dam project had been approved, and this small mountain community was posed for an exploding growth in population. With great boldness, the church changed their plans in order to provide room for this future growth. After construction had begun, the dam project was canceled. They had committed to build a sanctuary that would accommodate 1,000 and Sunday School space for well over 500 in a town of about 5,000. We had several classrooms that were actually locked up and not in use. One day I walked down the hallway looking at those empty rooms. I remember thinking, "Lord I'll never tell you again that I don't want to build." Lesson number three!

Soon after that I moved to First Baptist Church of Norfolk, and in our first seven years together, we have had no less than four major building programs. By the way, the final chapter concerning the facilities in Galax has not yet been written. God has a purpose for that space and a pastor who will lead the church to its productive use. I share this confessional testimony simply to say that we all have struggled with these issues of numbers and fellowship, but let me assure you that fellowship is not a factor of size.

The Nature of Biblical Fellowship (vv. 3-4)

We find in this text three characteristics of biblical fellowship. It is human, divine, and joyous. The word translated "fellowship" is *koinōnia*, the rich term we introduced in the last chapter. John declared that through the proclamation of the gospel we have a joint partnership with one another. Notice that John first mentioned the human dimension of fellowship that is "with us." Any claim to a vital relationship with God that does not find expression in human fellowship is a fraud. There is no such thing as lone-ranger Christianity in the New Testament. This letter is very pointed and specific concerning this matter.

John boldly declared that we can have assurance of our salvation because "we love the brethren" (1 John 3:14). He further described this love in terms of laying down one's life for the brethren (v. 16). Love will lead the believer to meet his brother's need (v. 17). If this brotherly love was lacking in the life of an individual, John concluded that the love of God also was absent. In the fourth chapter John stated this truth even more bluntly: "The one who does not love does not know God, for God is love" (4:8). John continued, "If someone says, 'I love God,' and hates his brother, he is a liar; for the one who does not love his brother whom he has seen, cannot love God whom he has not seen" (v. 20).

When we are born again, we are born into God's family. We enter into a brotherly relationship with others who are in Christ. Stephen Smalley has stated this truth well, "Christian fellowship is not the sentimental and superficial attachment of a random collection of individuals, but the profoundly mutual relationship of those who remain in Christ and therefore belong to each other."[3]

Second, our fellowship is with God and His Son. With this phrase John focused on fellowship in terms of its divine origin and empowering. This alone explains how believers can love one another. The strength of our fellowship comes from our divine connection with God Himself through His Son. It is the divine quality of our fellowship that breaks down the inner wall of partition.

Notice that this sharing of fellowship completes our joy (1:4). Joy, like love, is compounded as it is shared. Joy is characteristic of the Christian life. In John 15:11 Jesus told His disciples, "I have told you this so that my joy may be in you and that your joy may be complete" (NIV). Joy is the undergirding quality of the Christian life that overcomes circumstances because it comes from our union with Christ. As we share the gospel and thus enable others to embrace Christ, our joy is made complete. If there is one place in our community that should be known as a haven of joy, it should be the church. Is this true of your church or your Sunday School class?

Barriers to Fellowship (vv. 5-8)

If biblical fellowship is our calling and our heritage, why is it so seldom experienced in our local churches? There is indeed a barrier to fellowship, but it is not size. The barrier to fellowship is sin, unconfessed and unforgiven sin.

John declared a central truth of biblical revelation: "God is light" (1 John 1:5). The primary idea conveyed by the word *light* is the holiness of God. God is perfect holiness. John introduced the holiness of God in order to answer three false claims.

Claim	*Answer*
If we say that we have fellowship with Him and yet walk in the darkness, we lie (v. 6).	If we walk in the light . . . we have fellowship with one another, and the blood of Jesus His Son cleanses us (v. 7).
If we claim to be without sin, we deceive ourselves (v. 8, NIV).	If we confess our sins, He is faithful and righteous to forgive us our sins (v. 9).
If we say that we have not sinned, we make Him a liar (v. 10).	If anyone sins, we have an Advocate . . . and He Himself is the propitiation for our sins (2:1-2).

This entire section deals with both the ability of sin to destroy fellowship and the power of the blood of Christ to forgive sin.

John thundered an essential truth: we cannot have fellowship with God and live in sin. We know this truth from a practical standpoint. Anytime we tolerate the practice of sin in our lives, it disrupts our fellowship with God. We may claim anything we like with our mouths, but if we live in sin, we will not experience fellowship with God. Sin creates a barrier in our relationship with our Father.

I learned this truth the hard way as a young lad about seven years of age. My dad was my best friend and my hero as a little boy. (He still is!) I just enjoyed being with him no matter what he was doing. If he was mowing, I wanted to mow too. If he went to visit the hospitals, I wanted to go. Nothing could keep me from being with him. One day one of my older buddies brought home a pack of cigarettes. He wanted me to try a cigarette with him. Sin loves company! I didn't want to go with him because I knew what my dad thought of smoking, but I didn't want to be considered a sissy. We hid before we lit up. I took a few puffs to go along with the crowd, but as I inhaled the smoke, my heart filled with guilt and remorse. I had no more than put my first cigarette out than my mom called me for dinner. For the first time in my memory I didn't want to go home. I felt dirty. I just knew my dad would smell the cigarettes on my breath. I ran home and sneaked in the back door. I hustled to the bathroom, avoiding my parents. I claimed that I needed to wash my hands, but I actually wanted to do something to remove the smell of tobacco I knew must be clinging to my breath. I had seen adults gargle in order to have fresh breath. Unfortunately, I hadn't paid much attention to what they gargled. I got Mom's cologne rather than the mouthwash. Lilac breath isn't much better than tobacco. I was still conscious of my sin, and I was sure that my dad already knew. I was afraid to be near my dad because of my sin. Sin had destroyed for me the relationship that I cherished most. Sin blinds our eyes, hardens our heart, and alienates us from our Heavenly Father.

Sin not only destroys our fellowship with God, it has an impact on our relationship with others. Sin has a corporate effect. When I am out of fellowship with God, it affects my relationship to my wife and children and others around me. When I allow sin to place that barrier between God and myself, I lose my desire to fellowship with believers. Thus sin becomes that critical barrier to fellowship in the body of Christ. We see the effect of the sin of Ananias and Sapphira on the fellowship of the early church (Acts 5:1-11). Paul warned the Corinthians that their contentious, childish behavior was threatening to destroy the temple of God, that is, the church (1 Cor. 3:16-17). Sin alone has the power to alienate brother from brother. Sin is the one barrier to New Testament fellowship. Satan delights in using a critical, negative spirit to stop the work of the church and to destroy its fellowship. All around us we see churches crippled by dishonesty and distrust. Church splits are common in most communities. What a tragedy that the cause of the Kingdom itself is so adversely affected when fellowship fails.

Healing of Broken Fellowship (vv. 7-10)

What is the solution to this critical dilemma? We must walk in holiness as He is holy. Notice in verses 6-7 the logical flow of the argument. In verse 6 we are told that, if we say we have fellowship with God but practice sin, we lie. Sin thus affects our fellowship with the Father. Now in verse 7 we are instructed to walk in the light, but notice that the result of walking in the light is the restoration of our fellowship with one another. We might have expected John to say that walking in the light would restore fellowship with God, but John declared that to walk in the light led to fellowship with God's people. Our relationship to God and our fellowship with one another are intricately bound together. There is no way that I can be in perfect fellowship with God if I am not in fellowship with fellow believers. The idea that I'll just love God on my own and forget the church is utter nonsense. While salvation is a personal decision, it is a corporate experience. We are born into a family, and we grow in the context of that family.

The healing for broken fellowship is "the blood of Jesus" (v. 7). As we walk in the light, the sins of our lives will be clearly revealed to us, and our need for constant cleansing will be of first priority. The blood of Christ refers to the life of Christ freely given as the payment for our sin. The verb translated "cleanses" is in the present tense, which implies that it continually cleanses us of sin.

We must be honest at this point. If we attempt to maintain our innocence—"If we say that we have no sin"—we demonstrate that the truth is not in us. Anytime broken fellowship occurs, be it in a marriage or a Sunday School class, our defense mechanisms go up. We don't want to assume the blame, so we say things like "This is not my problem," "I didn't start it," or, "It's his fault." Ever hear these arguments from your children? They sound a lot like us, don't they? If we persist in our attempts to rationalize and explain away our sins, we'll never experience forgiveness. Furthermore, the broken fellowship in our lives and in our churches will not be healed.

We must get honest with God and with one another. Let's drop the facade. When we sin, we must stand ready to confess our sin and allow God's cleansing forgiveness to flow in our lives, in our relationships, and in our churches.

"Confess" is a key word. Somehow I used to have the mistaken idea that when I confessed my sin, I was revealing something to God that He did not know. Intellectually I knew that God was aware of my inmost thoughts, but practically I had not come to terms with that truth in my prayer life. Occasionally I harbored thoughts and attitudes that I didn't want anyone to know, not even God.

It took an event of personal forgiveness to help me to understand the meaning of confession. My brother is seven years older than I. Our childhood was marked by typical sibling rivalries. He enjoyed picking on me, and I made things worse with my little-brother whining and tattling. We shared the same bedroom, which made things more volatile. He often came in after I had gone to sleep, and he would wake me up just to annoy me. One night I was ready for him. I was loaded for big game. I had my basketball hidden beside the bed. If he woke me up, I was going to drill him with the basketball. My brother, Phil, came in from his date, and the rest of the household was already asleep. Sure enough, he was true to form. He woke me up just for the fun of it, but this time he woke me by pretending to kiss me good night. No thought could be more disgusting than a good-night kiss from a big brother. I sprang into action and launched my basketball for his head. He ducked! The ball sailed past him and broke the mirror in the wardrobe. In seconds, the unmistakable sound of Dad's footsteps was heard in the hallway. I jumped back into bed and pretended to be waking up from the sound of breaking glass. My brother had retrieved the ball and was standing before the broken mirror, ball in hand. Dad punished him and absolved me of the crime. What an exciting moment! I had finally gotten back at my big brother. I should have been enjoying this revenge, but I didn't. In fact I couldn't get back to sleep.

After rolling around for several agonizing minutes, I got up and made my feet carry me to Mom and Dad's bedroom. I was surprised to discover that Dad was still awake, apparently waiting for me to make this walk. "Dad," I blurted out, "I know you don't know this, but I threw the ball." There, it was done! I had confessed my awful sin, and now Dad knew everything.

Calmly he replied, "Son, I knew that all the time."

"You did?" I exclaimed. "Why didn't you spank me a while ago?"

"Because I wanted you to be able to tell me for yourself," he said.

That's what confession is all about. It comes from the Greek words *homo*, which means "same," and *logeo*, which means "to say." When we confess our sins, we agree with God about our sins. We agree that we have sinned, that sin disrupts our fellowship with God and people, and that Christ has paid the penalty for our sin. In response to our confession, God who is faithful and righteous both forgives our sin and grants purification from all unrighteousness. These words are beautifully expressive of two essential truths. God both releases us from sin and removes the stain of that sin.

Because sin has consequences in our human relationships, one further step remains. We must go to the brother or sister affected by our sin and make restitution. Remember that our Lord Himself commanded this action for the healing of fellowship. "If therefore you are presenting your offering at the altar, and there remember that your brother has something against you, leave your offering there before the altar, and go your way; first be reconciled to your brother, and then come and present your offering" (Matt. 5:23-24). Notice that this act of reconciliation takes precedence over worship. With eternity at stake in the ministry of the church, we cannot allow sin to create a barrier to fellowship and thus block the flow of God's power.

Perhaps this chapter has brought to mind areas of unconfessed, unforgiven sin in your life that are destroying your fellowship with God and your fellow Christians. Why not deal with them right now? Agree with God about your sin and experience the flow of His cleansing power.

Notes

1. Alexander Ross, *Commentary on the Epistles of James and John,* The New International Commentary (Grand Rapids: Wm. B. Eerdman Publishing Company, 1966), 136.

2. Stephen S. Smalley, *Word Biblical Commentary,* vol. 51, (Waco, Tex.: Word Books), 9.

3. Ibid., 12.

Crown Me

Let love be without hypocrisy. Abhor what is evil; cling to what is good. Be devoted to one another in brotherly love; give preference to one another in honor; not lagging behind in diligence, fervent in spirit, serving the Lord; rejoicing in hope, perservering in tribulation, devoted to prayer, contributing to the needs of the saints, practicing hospitality. Bless those who persecute you; bless and curse not. Rejoice with those who rejoice, and weep with those who weep. Be of the same mind toward one another; do not be haughty in mind, but associate with the lowly. Do not be wise in your own estimation. Never pay back evil for evil to anyone. Respect what is right in the sight of all men. If possible, so far as it depends on you, be at peace with all men. Never take your own revenge, beloved, but leave room for the wrath of God, for it is written, ''Vengeance is Mine, I will repay,'' says the Lord. ''But if your enemy is hungry, feed him, and if he is thirsty, give him a drink; for in so doing you will heap burning coals upon his head.'' Do not be overcome by evil, but overcome evil with good.

—Romans 12:9-21

My youngest daughter, Katie, loves to play her dad in checkers. She hasn't beaten me yet, but it's only a matter of time. I can remember playing checkers with my dad. He was good. I'm not sure if I ever beat him when he was playing at his hardest. I know that it's impossible to win at checkers without getting a king. The king can go in any direction. He is the king! It was always an exciting moment when I could slide my checker onto that back line and proudly declare, "Crown me!" It was such a good feeling to have a king.

Life has certain similarities to checkers. We like to be "crowned." We like authority because it lets us move wherever we choose. It lets us have our own way. Most people today seem to be bent on having their way. Yet the Bible tells us that biblical fellowship requires that we "give preference to one another in honor" (Rom. 12:10). Yet there are currents of influence in today's society that make it difficult to practice a self-giving life-style.

In the early seventies, Alvin Toffler wrote a book entitled *Future Shock* in which he described and predicted the effects of the constant and accelerating change that is a part of our culture. One of the effects of this constant change had to do with relationships with the people around us. Our relationships, he said, would be defined in functional terms. We would seek people out for what they could do for us. This would create disposable people. We need not entangle ourselves with others, we simply plug them in when they are useful. The end result would be an impersonal, functional society.

Another current of our modern-day society that merges with this stream of impersonalization and actually gives it greater strength is the "self" emphasis of popular psychology. A rash of books has been published, urging us to focus on our own needs. These books tell us that we must be our own best friends. If our spouses or family members get in the way of our personal self-fulfillment, we must look out for our own interests. Basic to this philosophy is the belief that happiness and human fulfillment are found in direct pursuit of one's own gratification. Thus our society has been rendered impersonal by the impact of constant change, and it has been made self-seeking and consumer oriented by the popular "self" psychology.

With two such strong currents of influence, the church faces a tremendous struggle in creating a climate of true biblical fellowship. When we read verses like Romans 12:10, we see how far society's ideals have moved from the biblical norm: "Be devoted to one another in brotherly love; give preference to one another in honor." But herein lies both the greatest challenge and greatest opportunity for the church. The challenge is to make biblical fellowship alive and practical. The opportunity lies in the very fact that many people are finding the impersonal consumer-oriented society to be terribly lonely and unfulfilling. They long for something more. They long for authentic fellowship. Unfortunately, many are turning to cultic groups to find their fellowship. For this reason we must take Paul's practical suggestions for fellowship with the utmost seriousness.

The Principle of Love

The primary characteristic of the individual believer and of the Christian community is love. The Greek word for *love* here is *agape. Agape* has already been used several times in earlier chapters of this letter (5:5, 8; 8:35, 39). In each of those cases, it refers to God's divine love for us. *Agape* describes a love that is undeserved on our part and unqualified on His. In Romans 8:28, Paul used a form of *agape* to speak of human love for God. Here in Romans 12 we are commanded to love the brethren with the quality of love with which God has loved us. Thus the Christian community is to be marked by a love that is more than thought or emotion. It is a love that combines word and deed without reservation and in an unconditional manner. This is an impossibility humanly speaking, but it is a mandate of the Spirit-controlled community.

Our community love is to be "without hypocrisy" (12:9). Our love is to be the real thing, the genuine article, and not something plastered on like a Sunday smile. The remainder of chapter 12 is virtually a commentary on the operation of pure love in the life of the believer. Paul then used two other Greek words to further describe the operation of *agape* in the Christian community. One of the words is *philadelphia,* which we recognize from the city of that name as brotherly love. The second word, *philostorgia,* is more unusual, occurring only here in the New Testament. It was used in contemporary Greek to denote tender family affection, like that of a mother's love for her own child. Thus we might paraphrase verse 10 as "love the brethren the way a mother loves and nurtures her own child." Our love must be tender, affectionate, and self-giving.

One aspect of this sort of genuine Christian love is that it will "abhor what is evil" and "cling to what is good" (v. 9). This appears to be a general exhortation. Christians are to hate and turn away from that which is evil and embrace the good. If we connect this general injunction with the call to genuine nurturing love, we can begin to understand the redemptive nature of our community affection. We abhor evil because we know that it is destructive to persons and thus to our fellowship and our mission. Remember there is only one barrier to fellowship: sin. Since we know that evil is always destructive, we must hate it. Many Christians avoid evil, but few really hate it. We often become apathetic to the effects of evil on our society, and we avoid it because we don't want to get involved. When evil affects our family members, we are already involved.

Let's think about this practically and apply it to our church fellowship. What should we do when we are let in on the most recent gossip or rumors. Sometimes, in the church, gossip is shared under the guise of a prayer concern. "I shouldn't tell you this, but I just want you to know how to pray." How do you respond when you hear gossip that clearly will be destructive. After we have grown spiritually, we don't want to be party to gossip; thus we refuse to repeat the juicy tidbit. Is that sufficient? If we abhor evil, should we not lovingly confront the person spreading the gossip? Should we not do our very best to stop the spread of this destructive cancer instantly? Perhaps we should encourage our brother or sister, who felt the need to share the gossip, to accompany us to visit the person being talked about. I know it sounds radical, but we are family!

Let's try a second one. What do you do when a critical spirit rears its head in your prayer group or Sunday School class. Someone begins to criticize the pastor or the deacons or the church itself. Do we just refuse to join in, or do we lovingly confront the destructive influence of this critical spirit? It is fascinating how a critical spirit spreads like oil on water.

A few years back I joined a well-known fitness center in our community. I visited several, but I chose this one because of the excellent services they offered. They kept the exercise machines in good repair, set the weights for the customer, and maintained very clean locker-room facilities. One day after a good workout I was sitting in the sauna with several other guys, none of whom I knew. As we were sweating together, one of the men started talking about how the service at the club had deteriorated. He complained about the locker rooms and the lack of space. He was quickly joined by the others in a veritable barrage of negativism. To hear them tell it, this place could do nothing right.

Soon the discussion turned to how good things used to be back during the good ole' days. These were the days before the fancy weight machines and colorful carpet. The more I listened, the worse the good ole' days actually sounded. I couldn't believe my ears. I had just joined because of the excellent service and fine facilities.

I began to think that I ought to say something, but it was none of my business. After a while I got tired of hearing this barrage of negativism. I plucked up my courage and said, "You know, I really like the service here." Dead silence! I continued, "Compared with other clubs I have visited, I think they do a fine job." An amazing thing occurred. After the initial shock wore off, one of the guys joined in with a word of praise, then another. Suddenly our gripe session became a praise session. We must be willing to challenge the evil of a critical destructive spirit in our churches and cling to the good.

Let's try a slightly harder example. If we truly hate evil and we know that someone in our class is involved in a destructive activity, do we simply ignore it because it is none of our business, and we don't want to get involved? Perhaps we know that a colleague at work is cheating on his wife; or we know that a friend is struggling with an addiction to alcohol, drugs, food, or even work. We listen to Charlie brag about his new boat that was purchased with money he made at his second job. Charlie wants the finer things of life; he's working every spare moment and neglecting his wife and children. You can see the signs that everything is about to come apart because you've been there. Do you turn a blind eye and fail to warn your Christian brother?

Now let's keep this matter balanced in our thinking. I'm not talking about starting a crusade to expose someone's sin before the whole church or Sunday School class. Remember we're talking about loving confrontation in the context of a community commanded to love one another unconditionally. A mother who saw destructive evil threatening the life of her child would lovingly confront the child but would never parade it before her neighbors.

We're part of a family where we must care enough to confront, and love enough to encourage and console our brothers and sisters as they work through their problems. It's a challenging thought I know, but if we can't discover love without hypocrisy in the life of the church, where can we find it?

Principle of Preference (vv. 10-12)

"Give preference to one another in honor." This idea must sound both radical and foreign to the pop psychologists of our day who insist on loving yourself first and sometimes exclusively. We should not think that this idea occurs only in this isolated text and, therefore, can be ignored. In Philippians 2:3-4, Paul developed the same idea. "Do nothing from selfishness or empty conceit, but with humility of mind let each of you regard one another as more important than himself; do not merely look out for your own personal interests, but also for the interests of others." Jesus taught a similar principle when He declared that in service there is true greatness.

What do we mean by giving preference in honor? Does it mean that we are to pretend that the other persons are right even if they are wrong? Do we simply act like others are better or wiser than we are? No, this has nothing to do with pretending or acting. Our love is without hypocrisy. We honor our brothers or sisters when we elevate their needs above our own. We are free to do this because we have discovered that in ministering to one another we are privileged to minister to the Lord Himself. The miracle of Christian community is that when we offer a cup of cold water to the thirsty brother, we have actually ministered unto our Lord (Matt. 25:34-40).

Do we give preference in practical matters, such as where we park or where we sit in church? Often growing churches have parking problems. Non-Christians are not likely to park away from the church and walk. The full parking lot gives them the excuse they need not to attend. Should the mature Christian choose to park at a further distance in order to reserve the closer places for visitors? At our church, rapid growth has created unique parking problems with only 595 spaces on site. Recently we inaugurated a "Preferred Parking Program," but with a Christian distinctive. When the world thinks of preferred parking, they mean parking right next to the door. In our case the preferred parking is in satellite lots a block away. We prefer to park away so that others can park near the church. Do we go to church business meetings with the sole intention of putting others' interests first? These are practical dimensions of biblical fellowship.

Putting others' needs first is not an attitude that comes easily or joyously for most folks. It can't be forced. All of us who are parents of young children have discovered this. For example, you invite your new neighbors over for the afternoon. They have a child the same age of your own. You envision a wonderful afternoon with the kids playing joyously together and the adults enjoying conversation. You introduce the children, and they run off excitedly to play together. After about five minutes of peace and quiet, your little one comes running in, tears streaming. After a few moments you discover the dilemma. Both children want to play with the scooter at the same time. You're embarrassed by the outburst of temper on the part of your child. You're frustrated because you know that your child hasn't looked at the scooter in six weeks. He probably had forgotten where he had thrown it. Now that the other child wants to play with it, your son wants it too. You're going to play the role of the peacemaker. "Johnny, why don't you share the scooter. Don't you want your new friend to use it first? You can play with it anytime you want."

"No! I want it. I want to play with it now."

Getting even more embarrassed, you excuse yourself and take Johnny into the bedroom. "Son, listen to me. If you don't share this toy, I'm going to punish you. I can't believe how selfishly you're behaving. Don't you know Jesus wants you to share?" We parents throw in a little theology to legitimize our discipline. "Now go back out there and let Freddie use the scooter first." Reluctantly, he wipes away the tears and heads back out.

"Here," he grunts with a scowl on his face, "You use the scooter first. Mom says I gotta share. Go ahead; take the old scooter."

That's not exactly what we had in mind. We wanted this lesson about sharing to be embraced a little more spontaneously, enthusiastically, and joyously.

Notice the collection of phrases in Romans 12:11-12 that further clarify the giving of preference to the brethren. First, Paul exhorted the Romans to do this in the following manner: "not lagging behind in diligence, fervent in spirit, serving the Lord" (v. 11). The giving of preference must be done with eagerness and diligence. This is not a forced compliance but a joyful opportunity to love the brethren. Because we are "serving the Lord" by giving preference to the brethren, there can be no room for apathy. We shouldn't try to get away with as little as possible, but we should seek opportunities to honor the brethren with unflagging zeal. This fervency for servanthood comes not by way of human temperament, but it is kindled in us by the power of the Holy Spirit. Thus we are "fervent in spirit." The real verification of the empowering of the Holy Spirit in our lives is not just bubbling religious emotionalism, but a spirit that leads us to love the brethren through selfless service.

While not all commentators would agree, I think the three phrases "rejoicing in hope, perservering in tribulation, devoted to prayer" (v. 12) describe the attitude necessary to love the brethren by showing preference. Servanthood is not an easy life-style, nor is it always well received. Therefore joy, perseverance, and prayer are essential ingredients to consistent servanthood. Joy, as we saw in the last chapter, is characteristic of Christian living (see Gal. 5:22). Our joy is able to persevere even in difficult circumstances because it has its source not in present circumstances, but in our future hope. This hope, Paul has already assured us (Rom. 5:5), will not disappoint, for it is the work of the Holy Spirit. Because our hope is sure, we can endure tribulation. Yet the daily empowering that keeps joy alive is prayer. It is this consistent communication with the Father that enables us to overcome discouragement and apathy in our service. The Gospels are full of examples of the power of prayer in the servant ministry of our Lord. Any attempt to make fellowship practical in our churches that does not find its focus in prayer is destined for failure. A popular bumper sticker declares: "The family that prays together, stays together." This truth well applies to the fellowship of the church.

The Principle of Physical Expression

Our love, if it is to be genuine, must include both word and deed. Contributing to the needs of the saints is one of the practical ways that we can build fellowship in our churches. As Christians we are to love even our enemies, yet we embrace fellow believers more closely. The spontaneous meeting of needs has been part and parcel of the church's makeup from the days of its inception. In Acts 2:44-45 we read: "All those who had believed were together, and had all things in common; and they began selling their property and possessions, and were sharing them with all, as anyone might have need." The presence of the Spirit prompts the sharing of our possessions and the meeting of physical needs in the life of the church. One of the great projects of Paul's ministry was the collection of the offering for the saints in Jerusalem who had been impoverished by a famine. Paul exhorted the Corinthians to complete their offering, reminding them that "at this present time your abundance being a supply for their want, that their abundance also may become a supply for your want, that there may be equality" (2 Cor. 8:14).

How the church goes about contributing to needs of the saints may vary from church to church depending both on the needs and resources. Many churches already have clothes closets, food pantries, and fuel assistance programs. In some communities these church-assistance programs have been decimated by yard sales. Perhaps we should ban yard sales and sacrifice the few dollars' profit for the sake of the needy. Increasingly, the church is being confronted with the needs of those who are temporarily unemployed. The plight of senior adults on fixed income cannot go unnoticed. Of course, we must expand our vision to the worldwide needs of our family. Many of our brothers and sisters in Christ in other parts of the world are facing starvation, not just temporary financial difficulties. These folks too are family. We must honestly face this practical matter of fellowship. If we are to experience true *koinōnia*, it must express itself in a practical fashion. There are no easy answers, but this must be addressed by local churches, denominations, and by the entire Christian community.

We often run across a barrier to the practical expression of fellowship. Often our own members are too proud or too embarrassed to ask for and receive help. I know this presents a practical problem for many churches. This fact should demonstrate how far we have to go in building genuine fellowship. We must strive for a family atmosphere in which honesty prevails and pride does not block the flow of the Spirit.

A second practical method of expressing fellowship in the New Testament era was the practice of hospitality. The need for housing was very acute in New Testament days for believers who had to travel outside their own area. Recall, too, that the early churches had no buildings; therefore, they depended on hospitality for meetings for worship. In Acts we are told that they were "breaking bread from house to house, they were taking their meals together with gladness and sincerity of heart" (2:46). In 1 Peter 4:9, we are commanded: "Be hospitable to one another without complaint." The phrase "without complaint" suggests that hospitality opens us to the risk of abuse and disappointment. This is true concerning nearly every area of practical fellowship. The danger of abuse does not absolve us from the command to practice hospitality.

Does this need exist in our day? Hospitality may be an even more pressing need in the midst of growing impersonalization. We might think about the needs of single members of our church who are living away from home, particularly during holidays. We must be careful to include families in fellowship activities who are presently missing a parent for any reason. In our area military families abound. Frequently a new family moves into our community, and the husband leaves for sea duty. In those cases the remaining family members hunger for hospitality. We might consider opening our homes to an unwed mother who has been forced out of her own home. If your church is in a college town, think about the needs of the college students. A singles ministry provides numerous opportunities for married couples to open their homes for fellowship to single adults. At the most basic level, we should invite other church families over for fellowship. If we want to develop genuine fellowship in our churches, we must open our homes.

Principle of Mutual Relationships (vv. 14-21)

A majority of commentators argue that with verse 14 Paul turned his attention to the relations of Christians with those outside the church. This view has been prompted by the mention of persecution and the use of the word *enemy* in verse 20. This majority view is not without its problems. For example, verses 15 and 16 can be understood only in the context of Christian community. The believer cannot possibly be of "one mind" with the unbeliever. I personally think that Paul was still addressing the issue of practical fellowship. If we are honest, we will admit that we are not perfect and, therefore, our churches are not perfect. Thus our fellowship is not without its glitches. What happens when we are hurt by a fellow believer?

These instructions should not surprise us. One of the inevitable features of family living is conflict. As a pastor I am involved in premarital counseling. During one of the counseling sessions I talk about how to deal with conflict. I am always slightly amused when a couple sweetly smiles and replies, "Pastor, we don't need this; we never fight." I don't try to burst their bubble. I just tell them to take notes anyway; they might need them for someone else. Because we are all different, conflict does occasionally happen. How do we resolve conflict so as to enrich our fellowship? Verse 14, "Bless those who persecute you; bless and curse not" serves as something of a summary for this entire section. As Christians we not only refrain from desiring harm for those persecuting us, but we actually desire good for them. We pray that God will bless them.

In Christ, we actually become one body, so much so that we feel one another's pain and joy. When we stub our toes, and it hurts, our whole body feels the pain. When one of our members experiences pain and weeps, we should all weep. The idea here is that we actually stand beside one another in fellowship so much that we feel the pain and experience the joy.

Paul continued his train of thought by calling the Roman Christians to be of the same mind toward one another. In Philippians 2:2, Paul challenged his readers to have the same mind, and that mind he described as the mind of Christ. When we have the mind of Christ, we will be of one mind with the brethren. It is thus a calling to humility and servanthood. Here in Romans 12 Paul warned the Romans against an arrogance that would cause them to break fellowship with those who they consider to be lowly. In Christ there is no place for a feeling of superiority; we are all the recipients of "grace" (see Rom. 12:3). No one is lowly, unimportant, or ordinary in Christ. Therefore, Paul reminded the Romans that they must not be wise in their own estimation. Self-styled wisdom and importance are destructive to fellowship and therefore a hindrance to the church's mission.

Very likely in verse 16 Paul had in mind a specific conflict in Rome. Chapters 14 and 15 contain a detailed treatment of a controversy involving the weak and the strong. The controversy had to do with the eating of certain foods and the observing of special days of worship. "One man has faith that he may eat all things, but he who is weak eats vegetables only" (14:2).

"One man regards one day above another, another regards every day alike" (14:5). Paul didn't choose one side against the other; rather, he encouraged them to stop judging one another and determine to build up the fellowship. "For if because of food your brother is hurt, you are no longer walking according to love. Do not destroy with your food him for whom Christ died" (14:15). "So then let us pursue the things which make for peace and the building up of one another" (14:19).

Some in Rome tended to consider brothers and sisters as weaker Christians if they did not share particular convictions about food or worship. Such spiritual arrogance created stumbling blocks to fellowship. They were not to overevaluate their wisdom but to strive for that which would edify the brethren.

Practical Ways to Defuse Evil

Paul concluded this chapter with a practical methodology for defusing evil. These are practical suggestions that can be applied in your home as well as your church.

Don't return evil for evil to anyone (v. 17)

The first step in defusing evil is the absolute refusal to participate in evil. The believer simply refuses to deal in kind. It's hard to fight when the other party refuses to show up. Christians are to seek those things that are good (see 12:9). We are the arbiters of peace in the world.

Initiate the peace talks (v. 18)

The phrases "if possible" and "so far as it depends on you" (12:18) warn us that true peace requires reconciliation of both parties. Some people won't let us establish peace. That does not provide an excuse for us to fail to initiate the peace talks. We must take the initiative in seeking peace.

Don't play God (v. 19)

When we take revenge, we are playing God. Only God is perfectly holy; only God is qualified to bring vengeance. Paul quoted the first part of Deuteronomy 32:35 in confirmation of this truth: Vengeance is Mine, and retribution,/In due time their foot will slip;/For the day of their calamity is near,/And the impending things are hastening upon them. Vengeance was prohibited in the Old Testament because it is God's prerogative alone. We must note that this matter of vengeance has universal application. This is true both inside and outside the Christian community. Have you ever hit back at someone verbally only to discover later that you didn't have all the facts? Later, you wish you could retrieve your vengeful words. Simply refuse to play God's role in handing out vengeance.

Overcome evil with good (vv. 20-21)

In the place of vicious retaliation, we are to bring active good will. Here Paul quoted Proverbs 25:21-22: If your enemy is hungry, give him food to eat;/And if he is thirsty, give him water to drink;/For you will heap burning coals on his head. It is not enough to refrain from evil. As people called to be peacemakers, we are to express every sort of kindness to those who treat us as enemies. We don't respond in this way in the joyful anticipation that the Lord will punish our enemies. The purpose of our loving goodwill is to bring our enemies to repentance and thus overcome evil with good. The curious picture of the heaping of live coals on one's head apparently referred to a ritual whereby people repented of their offenses by carrying a dish containing burning charcoal on their heads.[1]

The victory of the Christian fellowship is complete when repentance is achieved and fellowship is restored. The biblical concept of showing preference to the brethren is certainly radical. It goes against the grain of our own desires and popular thinking. It is only possible by the empowering of the Spirit. The modern-day church has drifted far from the biblical ideal. For the sake of the gospel, we must move forward to embrace those principles of genuine love.

When fellowship becomes real and we lose our desire to cry out "crown me," we will discover a freedom that only the Spirit can give. Biblical fellowship will transform your life and that of your church.

Notes

1. C. E. B. Cranfield, *A Commentary of Romans 12-13*, Scottish Journal of Theology Occasion of Papers, vol. 12, (London: Oliver Boyd, 1965), 55-60.

8

Let's Play Wedding

Therefore, gird your minds for action, keep sober in spirit, fix your hope completely on the grace to be brought to you at the revelation of Jesus Christ. As obedient children, do not be conformed to the former lusts which were yours in your ignorance, but like the Holy One who called you, be holy yourselves also in all your behavior; because it is written, "You shall be holy, for I am holy." And if you address as Father the One who impartially judges according to each man's work, conduct yourselves in fear during the time of your stay upon earth; knowing that you were not redeemed with perishable things like silver or gold from your futile way of life inherited from your forefathers, but with precious blood, as of a lamb unblemished and spotless, the blood of Christ. For He was foreknown before the foundation of the world, but has appeared in these last times for the sake of you who through Him are believers in God, who raised Him from the dead and gave Him glory, so that your faith and hope are in God.
—1 Peter 1:13-21

I hated to hear the suggestion, "Let's play wedding." As a young man I considered this game even more objectionable than playing house. What self-respecting boy could imagine wanting to marry a girl! Marriage and weddings were the furthest thing from my mind. But in my neighborhood one had little choice. There weren't enough guys to have a good game of baseball without the help of the girls. Thus for the sake of fairness, we had to play "wedding" once in a while. After all, the girls did play baseball earlier in the day, and we were planning on another game later in the afternoon.

Our moms were only too happy to help by donating old clothes to dress the wedding party. The bride and groom were suitably attired, with the bride in white. Thus the wedding was ready to commence. I always wanted to be the preacher. That way there was no "yucky" wedding kiss. Besides, I thought it was fun to marry someone "in holy macaroni."

Play weddings were to be tolerated, not anticipated, by a boy. But real weddings? They're something special. They are joyous occasions. There are the days of planning and anticipation. Countless details must be attended to. There are the showers to attend, the invitations must be mailed, the florist has to be called, the planning with the pastor is a necessity, and, of course, we can't forget to meet with the caterer. The day finally arrives replete with jangled nerves and sleepless, anxious nights. The actual wedding, when it is past, is little more than a blur. Perhaps this explains why it is so difficult to decide which pictures to omit, and we end up buying more than we can afford.

Many couples are surprised to discover that the wedding itself contains so many traditional symbols—from the unity candle to the rings to the garter. For most brides, the truly significant symbol is the wedding gown itself. It is pure white, often with glistening sequins and delicate lace. Certainly the gown is the most expensive and perhaps even the most impractical of the symbols. Most wedding dresses are rarely worn again, unless they are passed down to a fortunate daughter or granddaughter. But few brides are willing to compromise when it comes to this symbol. The wedding gown speaks of the bride's purity and of the holiness of the marriage commitment.

One of the pastor's primary duties is to ensure that the groom gets into the sanctuary without fainting. I usually encourage the groom just to stand beside me at the altar and focus his attention on that center aisle. In a moment he will behold a picture that forever will be etched on his mind. His bride will appear in all of her beauty. He will never have seen her look so lovely. She will be glowing radiantly, her natural beauty set off and enhanced by the gown: the symbol of her purity, her holiness.

A Comparison

In Ephesians, Paul compared marriage with Christ's love for His church:

> Husbands, love your wives, just as Christ also loved the church and gave Himself up for her; that He might sanctify her, having cleansed her by the washing of water with the word, that He might present to

Himself the church in all her glory, having no spot or wrinkle or any such thing; but that she should be holy and blameless (5:25-27).

The church is called to wear white, to be the precious, holy bride of Christ Himself. We, as the church, have been called to uncompromised holiness!

Yet this vision for a holy church has nearly been lost. The church has become so distorted by sin that we are almost afraid to preach the demand for holiness. As a result we are anything but pure. The ravages of sin have pockmarked the church, and we scarcely make any impression on our secular environment. There are those who want to object that until the Lord returns there will be sin in the church. Even if we must agree with this observation, we must object to the implication: since there will be sin, let's not worry about it or preach holiness!

We must preach holiness and strive for the upward call of God in Christ Jesus. Holiness is the precondition for fellowship. Fellowship, as we have seen, is essential to the proper working of the body. Some historians have argued that churches of past centuries focused too much on purity to the exclusion of other matters. While that may be true, I would suggest that churches of today have ignored it in our preoccupation with the running of programs, the accomplishment of social ministries for the good of our communities, and the construction of buildings. The call to holiness must be heard if the church is going to make a significant impact on our secular society.

The Context of Holiness: Our Birthright

The apostle Peter wrote, "Like the Holy One who called you, be holy yourselves also in all your behavior; because it is written, 'You shall be holy, for I am Holy' " (1 Pet. 1:15-16). Peter quoted a phrase that was virtually a refrain of the Book of Leviticus (11:44; 19:2; 20:7,26). Basically, *holy* means "separate" or "marked off." In the Old Testament, God Himself is understood as the Holy One. He is the source of true holiness. The Hebrew people, because of the unique personal relationship with the Holy One, were themselves "separated" unto Him. It is God Himself who imparts holiness to the objects or people that He calls unto Himself. For that reason Jerusalem is holy (Isa. 48:2), as was the Temple in that place (Isa. 64:10). The priests and the vessels in the Temple were to be holy for

service unto the Holy One. Thus, holiness is positively a separation unto God for His service. We cannot, however, neglect the
following truth that persons separated unto God for His use
must also be separated from sin because God is holy. Thus the
context for understanding our call to holiness is in our personal
relationship with Holy God.

The first chapter of 1 Peter begins with a look at our redemption. Just look at these critical phrases:

verse 3: "born again to a living hope"
verse 4: "to obtain an inheritance which is imperishable and
   undefiled"
verse 5: "protected by the power of God through faith for
   a salvation ready to be revealed in the last time"
verse 7: "faith, . . . more precious than gold which is perishable"
verse 8: "you greatly rejoice with joy inexpressible"
verse 9: "obtaining as the outcome of your faith the salvation
   of your souls."

Peter concluded this wonderful section by telling us that our
salvation was such that the prophets made a careful search and
inquiry (v. 10), but they could only predict it. They discovered
that they were not serving themselves but *us*. My favorite
expression is in verse 12. Our redemption was so precious that
even the angels desired to obtain a clear look. Can you picture
the angels peering over the side of heaven to see the precious
plan of redemption made available to us? Because we are born
again by an imperishable seed, because we are now children
of God Himself, we have a new birthright. We must be like our
Father who is holy. This is not optional; it is the natural consequence of our new birth.

The Call of Holiness: Our Service

Holiness and redemption, cannot be separated. In verse 13,
Peter began with "Therefore," which forces the reader to see
the present demand in light of the truths just discussed. Because of the glorious truth of our redemption, we are called to
action. Salvation implies service, and service demands holiness. Peter first spelled out four things that must be done by
the believer in preparation for service. Many scholars have
suggested that this fourfold direction originally may have been

given in the context of baptism. This would give it an even more solemn and lasting impression.

Mental Preparedness

The first command is "gird your minds for action" (v. 13). The picture is that of the Eastern man gathering up his long, flowing robe and tucking it into·his belt so as to free his legs for action. When a man prepared to run or to fight a battle, he would tuck his robe in his belt. For example, in 1 Kings we find the story of the prophet Elijah who had prayed for rain to end the drought in Israel. When the small cloud appeared, he warned Ahab to prepare his chariot and go down so that the coming heavy rain would not stop him. The text then recorded Elijah's actions, "Then the hand of the Lord was on Elijah, and he girded up his loins and outran Ahab to Jezreel" (1 Kings 18:46).

Christians are called to gird up their minds in preparation for service. The mind is used in the sense of that which guides and dictates conduct. Paul warned us that the spiritual battle is fought in the mind: "We are destroying speculations and every lofty thing raised up against the knowledge of God, and we are taking every thought captive to the obedience of Christ" (2 Cor. 10:5). If we believe that we can fill our minds with impure, jealous, or envious thoughts and still be holy, we are fooling ourselves. We must, therefore, be cautious about what we take into our mind through our senses if we are going to be fit for service. Christians should carefully evaluate the movies or television they watch. We must carefully monitor the message of the music to which we listen. We must be discerning about the conversations we participate in. If we constantly input thoughts that lead us to such feelings as selfishness, envy, lust, or anxiety, they will affect our behavior. We cannot input impurity and expect to output holiness.

Positively, we must fill our minds with the Word of God, with pure and lovely thoughts. Paul constantly emphasized the need for mental preparedness. "Set your mind on the things above, not on the things that are on earth" (Col. 3:2). "Finally, brethren, whatever is true, whatever is honorable, whatever is right, whatever is pure, whatever is lovely, whatever is of good repute, if there is any excellence and if anything worthy of praise, let your mind dwell on these things" (Phil. 4:8). Thus, the first step to holiness is mental preparedness. We must become serious about guarding and feeding our minds. In many cases, Christians, churches, and even denominations have neglected the basics of prayer, Bible study, and Scripture memorization. Church is no game, and these priorities cannot be neglected if we're going to be prepared for service. We must improve the level of Bible study in our churches. We must teach our people how to study the Bible for themselves. We must rediscover the power of prayer. We don't need another program; we need to start practicing the basics.

Spiritual Balance

The second step to prepare for service is to "keep sober in spirit." "Sober" is a favorite term of the writer (see 4:7; 5:8). The idea is that of temperance or a disciplined behavior that avoids extremes. It is a Christian life characterized by self-control. Actual drunkenness was considered as a return to non-Christian ways, and it is rebuked in 1 Peter 4:3. In this verse, however, Peter was calling for a spiritual balance in all of our life-styles that comes from discipline. The most neglected aspect of church life in our day is the disciplines of regular prayer and Bible study in the home. George Gallup, in a speech delivered at the 1987 Lausanne Committee for World Evangelization, said: "Americans need help with the "how to" aspects of faith—how to pray. Those who do the most to live the Christian message invariably have a deep, steady prayer life, but most Americans have not developed such a life."[1] The discipline of regular Sunday School and worship attendance is a forgotten priority. The writer to the Hebrews warned his readers not to forsake the assembling together (10:25). This is a matter of spiritual discipline. Without spiritual self-control, the quest for holiness is merely wishful thinking.

Proper Perspective

The third imperative involves our perspective on life itself: "Fix your hope completely on the grace to be brought to you at the revelation of Jesus Christ" (1 Pet. 1:13). We are called to keep a long-term perspective on life. If we talk with mature investors, they will caution us to invest with a long-term perspective. Those who try to time the market on Wall Street and jump in and out often get burned. Those who invest with the perspective of fifteen or twenty years can tolerate the shocks of a market drop without panic and ride the highs without arrogance.

The Christian is called to keep a long-term perspective on life itself. If we live our present life in terms of the sure return of holiness, it will transform our present behavior. Only eternity gives purpose to the present-day experiences, whether they be suffering (see 1:6) or the enjoyment of abundance. When we begin to think about our daily lives and everyday decisions in light of God's eternal purpose in our lives, it leads inevitably to holy living.

Obedience: The Key

"As obedient children, do not be conformed to the former lusts which were yours in your ignorance, but like the Holy One who called you, be holy yourselves also in all your behavior" (vv. 14-15). We really don't like to listen to the key word of this text, but listen we *must*. You were chosen by God and sanctified by the Spirit "that you may obey Jesus Christ" (v. 2). Obedience, the fourth step, enables us to overcome the lustful passions that controlled our lives before our salvation. Obedience was the key to Jewish ethics, and it is indeed central to Christian maturity and holiness. In this letter alone the word *obedience* is given great emphasis (1:22; 2:13,18; 3:1; and 5:5). Everybody seems to be looking for a shortcut to Christian maturity, a quick fix for holiness. No shortcut exists. Obedience is the characteristic of the believer on the way to holiness.

The Why's of Holiness

When you're listening to someone preach, do you ever want to yell out "Why?" Why do we need to be holy? Is this just another legalistic, puritanical concept placed on us to repress our natural desires and squelch our fun? You would think so, sometimes, when you hear people talk about holiness. For instance, "Everything I enjoy is either fattening or sinful!" What a distortion of reality. Holiness is actually the path to joy and fulfillment. There are several good reasons that we need to be holy. Peter gave us three.

Because of the Judgment (v. 17)

The first reason is the privilege to address God as Father. We cannot take this privilege lightly. We can find Old Testament references where God is referred to as Father, but the New Testament community probably derived its use of "Father" from Jesus. He spoke to God as Father in a new and intimate manner. He instructed His disciples to pray "Our Father who art in heaven" (Matt. 6:9). This address became so characteristic of the early Christian community that we find it preserved in its Aramaic form "Abba" in Romans 8:15 and Galatians 4:6.

To call God "Father" is not simply privilege; it implies responsibility. Our Father is the one who judges impartially. The fact that God is our Father does not alter the fact that He is the righteous Judge. In fact, the writer of Hebrews pointedly said that a good father chastens his children (Heb. 12:5-11).

As Judge God is impartial, and in the present context that means He must also judge His children. We don't like to talk about the judgment of believers. It's about as popular a topic in the church today as is holiness. We must, however, acknowledge this biblical truth. Believers will one day stand before Holy God in judgment. In Romans 14:10-12 Paul wrote: "For we shall all stand before the judgment seat of God. For it is written, 'As I live says the Lord, every knee shall bow to Me,/ And every tongue shall give praise to God.' So then each one of us shall give account of himself to God." In 1 Corinthians 3:10-15, Paul painted an unforgettable picture of judgment when he depicted Christians as builders who are constructing through their deeds. Paul declared that one day fire will test the quality of our work. If it remains, we shall receive a reward; but if it is consumed, we shall suffer loss. We tend to overlook the truth that one day a Holy God will hold us accountable for our life's work.

I can never think of the concept of the judgment of believers without thinking back to my days of college football at Wake Forest. The day we looked forward to all week was Saturday, the day of the game. Sometimes during the week practice became somewhat boring and tedious. There was a tremendous temptation to slack off. If you were careful, you could loaf without being caught. You could give 75 percent rather than 100 percent. On the day of the game, you often knew you weren't at your most competitive edge because of your lack of work and preparation during the week. What was interesting is that this was not always evident to the fans. Frequently, fans could be fooled by one or two good plays. They simply were not perceptive enough to really see the poor quality of the overall performance. The player himself was usually aware of the quality of his own play. Often the postgame adulations were soothing. You would console yourself thinking, *Maybe I didn't play such a bad game.* But then came Sunday afternoon and the dreaded "films." That's right; everything was recorded in living color. Films don't lie! There was the agonizing truth— in slow motion! The projector reran our mistakes before our very eyes, and judgment was assured.

We sometimes grow casual about our spiritual lives and about our holiness. We can "play the church game" sufficiently well to fool most people, but we must recognize that God is not fooled. One day we must stand in judgment before Holy God. We are called to holy living *now.* God's desire is that we will be privileged to hear the words "well done . . . good and faithful servant" (Matt. 25:21, KJV). For that very reason, He calls us to holy living in the present.

Because of the cost of our redemption (vv. 18-19)

The picture changes from God as Judge to God as Redeemer. Secondly, we are called to holy living because of the very cost of our redemption. Nothing as cheap as silver and gold paid the price of our redemption. The precious blood of the Lamb of God, Christ Himself, paid the penalty for our sins. Christ's death is seen here as an obedient sin offering. Since the "wages of sin is death," silver and gold would be worthless in the redemption of humankind. Christ Himself, through His sacrificial death, was able to grant us true forgiveness. Our youth enjoy singing a little chorus that summarizes well the thought of this verse:

> He paid a debt He did not owe,
> I owed a debt I could not pay.
> I needed someone to wash my sins away.
> And now I sing a brand new song,
> Amazing Grace all day long.
> Christ Jesus paid the debt that I could not pay.

Jesus' death delivered us from the "futile" or powerless inheritance from our forefathers and enables us to live lives of abundant holiness. The word "futile" probably indicates that many of the recipients of this letter had been pagans. Their worship of idols and false gods had been "futile" and had left them hopeless. Actually, any life that is not based on Christ is futile and powerless. It stands to reason that anything less than obedient holiness would be insignificant, given the cost of redemption. For the church and its individual members to conduct themselves in a manner other than true holiness brings reproach on the sacrifice paid to grant redemption and secure our holiness.

Because of the Eternal Nature of our Fellowship (v. 22)

Some readers of this text miss the obvious connection between holiness and fellowship. If you will recall our study of 1 John 1:1-9, we actually anticipated this point. Thirdly, if sin is the barrier to fellowship, then it would follow that holiness is the path to fellowship. Our spiritual birth should not only result in maturing holiness, but it also should result in a growing love for fellow believers. The desire for biblical fellowship must emerge from the genuine new birth experience.

We should notice here that holiness is not some inner, private experience intended to minister to the needs of the one purified. This seems to me where many have missed the point of holiness. Holiness should never cause us to withdraw from the community or isolate ourselves. It should not create a holier-than-thou barrier that separates an individual from other believers. Holiness should lead to the edification of the community. It is a social experience, not just an individualistic one.

The phrase "purified your souls" (v. 22) translates a perfect participle. The tense implies an event in the past whose efforts continue. Likely, Peter was referring to the public act of baptism. He was not suggesting that the act of baptism itself purifies, but it does give visible testimony to the purification that God gives because of our response in salvation (see 1 Pet. 3:21).

Now notice that we were purified with a specific purpose in mind: "Since you have in obedience to the truth purified your souls for a sincere love of the brethren, fervently love one another from the heart" (1:22). "Sincere" translates the same

Greek word that Paul used in Romans 12:9 to call the Romans to a genuine love of the brethren. Peter underlined the thought once more with the phrase "fervently love one another from the heart." The idea is an unfailing love that comes from a commitment to be loving whatever the circumstances.

Many forces tended to divide the early Christian community. Natural barriers were created by Jew-Gentile, slave-free, male-female distinctions, and barriers emerged from the heretical teachings. No doubt the most difficult barriers to fellowship then and now were those that came from human sinfulness, which produced malice, guile, hypocrisy, envy, and slander (2:1). For this reason, holiness is the foundation for true fellowship in the life of the church.

Peter ended this section with an emphasis on the imperishable nature of the Word of God that produced our redemption and thus established the church. The point is well made. The seed whereby we were born again is imperishable; it is the "living and abiding word of God" (1:23). It is this implanted, imperishable seed that fertilizes the egg of our response and produces new life, which is in its very nature imperishable. We are God's *forever* family, and, therefore, we must of necessity learn to love one another here on earth. We will spend eternity together.

Our situation today is not all that different from that of the New Testament church. We still have racial, social, and cultural barriers. We fight the influence of divisive false teaching. And human nature is still the same. Hypocrisy, malice, and many other carnal attitudes continue to disrupt our fellowship. The solution has not changed! We must in obedience to the truth allow God to continually purify us for the love of the brethren. We must hunger for this intimate fellowship and personal holiness with all our heart.

The "How-to" of Holiness

Too much is at stake in the ministry of the church for us to be casual about this matter of holiness. Thus our obvious question must be, "How do we seek holiness?" The "therefore" of 2:1 ties the direction of these early verses to the call to holiness.

Put Aside Sin That Hinders Fellowship

To be holy some things must be put aside. If we think we can grow in holiness without "putting aside" (2:1) sin that hinders us from loving one another, we are deceiving ourselves. Paul used a similar imagery in Colossians 3:8-10 and Ephesians 4:22-24. Likely the image of "putting aside" and putting on was taken from the picture of baptism where the candidate took off old clothes and emerged from the water in beautiful, clean new robes.

Peter looked specifically at sins that would be disruptive to fellowship. "Malice" is a comprehensive term that includes all wickedness, and thus it serves as somewhat of a general heading for guile, hypocrisy, envy, and slander. "Guile" refers to words that are spoken to deceive. "Hypocrisy" is the wearing of a mask. It is a parading of outward conduct intended only to impress. Therefore, it is not genuine. "Envy" is a jealous striving that comes from a desire to have what another possesses. Envy would thus destroy the body that rejoices together. If I desire what you have, I cannot rejoice at your good fortune. "Slander" is words intended to hurt that often arise from our envy of another. Notice that Peter dealt with specific sins. We often are vague in our attempts to put away sin in general. We must fight against the individual specific sins in our lives that destroy our relationship with Holy God and our fellowship with one another.

Long for the Word

Notice the order of this passage. The putting away of sin precedes growth "in respect to salvation." Sin in our lives destroys our appetites for God's Word. It creates a vicious cycle! Sin destroys fellowship with God and one another, and then it dulls our appetites for God's Word, prayer, and gathered worship: the very sources where healing for sin is discovered. To break out of this sin cycle that dulls our appetite for God's Word, we must put aside the sins that keep us from holy living. While purification is logically first, purification and growth are inextricably bound together and are, therefore, both continuous.

The believer is to "long for the pure milk of the word" (2:2). Any parent of a newborn understands the point of this illustration. When your newborn's ear-piercing cry penetrates the household at 2:00 in the morning, you know that nothing will satisfy the infant other than milk. Rocking and cuddling do not suffice when the baby longs for milk. We must realize that nothing will satisfy the deep spiritual hunger of the born-again believer other than the milk of God's Word. This hunger for the Word of God is a sure sign of the new birth. Obviously, milk is not to be taken in a literal sense but as a symbol of spiritual food that provides for the spiritual growth. Therefore, we need not press the details of the picture.

Christians do not outgrow their need for milk as they mature, as a baby might outgrow its need for mother's milk. The milk here is Christ Himself who is the Word of God. This is seen from 2:3. Believers have already tasted the kindness of the Lord; therefore, they hunger to continue to drink of the pure milk. Ernest Best pointed out that the English translation conceals the full impact of 2:3. The verse contains a play on words. The Greek word for "kindness" is *chrēstos*. If we simply alter the vowel, we have *christos*, the Greek word for Christ. Best translated this verse, "you have tasted that the Lord is good (=Christ)," i.e. good for food, for growth.[2]

It is equally true that we feed upon Christ through our spiritual disciplines. We encounter the living Word through the written Word. If we look back at 1:23-25, we find mention of the imperishable Word. That word is defined as "the word which was preached to you" (v. 25). Thus the gospel, the written Word, is that which reveals the living Word. If we desire to grow in holiness, we must be willing to spend time in prayer and personal Bible study. We must long for this time with the Lord with the intensity that a baby longs for milk. To say we desire holiness is one thing; to seek it with a passionate hunger is quite another. We are called to holiness, but we will not grow in holiness until we are willing to put "aside" evil and long for our time of fellowship with God.

If the church were to recover this emphasis on holiness and purity, it would greatly enhance our effectiveness. It would solidify our fellowship and empower our witness. It begins with individual members who are willing to be obedient children in seeking after holiness in all our behavior.

We cannot play wedding, for we are truly the bride of Christ.

Notes

1. George Gallup, "Worldwide Trends in Religion" (Speech given at the Biennial Meeting of the Lausanne Committee for World Evangelization, Atlanta, 22 January 1987), 12.

2. Ernest Best, *1 Peter* (Grand Rapids: Wm. B. Eerdmans, 1971), 99.

9

Play Your Wild Card

And coming to Him as to a living stone, rejected by men, but choice and precious in the sight of God, you also, as living stones, are being built up as a spiritual house for a holy priesthood, to offer up spiritual sacrifices acceptable to God through Jesus Christ. For this is contained in Scripture:

"Behold I lay in Zion a choice stone, a precious corner stone,

And he who believes in Him shall not be disappointed." This precious value, then, is for you who believe. But for those who disbelieve,

"The stone which the builders rejected,

This became the very corner stone," and,

"A stone of stumbling and a rock of offense"; for they stumble because they are disobedient to the word, and to this doom they were also appointed. But you are a chosen race, a royal priesthood, a holy nation, a people for God's own possession, that you may proclaim the excellencies of Him who has called you out of darkness into His marvelous light; for you once were not a people, but now you are the people of God; you had not received mercy, but now you have received mercy.

—1 Peter 2:4-10

Many games have some token that serves as a wild card. Once drawn, this card or token is held until the conditions of the game merit its use. It is a card that carries privilege without responsibility. When the opportune moment occurs, I can play my wild card, and it can save the day for me.

Many Christians today view the idea of the priesthood of believers in much the same way that they do a "wild" card: all privilege without responsibility. We appear to "play" our "wild" card when it seems most convenient to our cause with little attention to it at other times. Does the priesthood of believers mean that I have the right to interpret the Bible however I choose and without regard to the historic belief of my church or denomination? Am I using priesthood of believers like a wild card when I interpret it in terms of authority to obstinately vote in a church meeting as I choose, without due regard for the interest of others? Does priesthood of believers represent nothing more than my right to pray without any human intercessor? When I hear the doctrine of the priesthood of believers being discussed, the emphasis is on privilege more often than responsibility. Let's look a little more carefully at this cherished biblical idea.

Holiness Relates to Service

In the last chapter we considered the call to be holy like our Father. In this chapter we will look at the implications of holiness as it relates to our service in the body of Christ. Peter utilized three separate Old Testament images in chapter 2 to illustrate the believer's responsibility and privilege for ministry in the body of Christ. The image of a temple made up of living stones pictures the vital growing nature of the New Testament church. The royal priesthood points to the believer's service or ministry within the temple. The responsibility to witness to the living God is represented by the notion of a "people for God's own possession."

A Holy Temple (vv. 4-5)

The basic picture of the entire section is that of a spiritual house or temple where acceptable sacrifices are offered up to God through Jesus Christ. This idea is consistent with Paul's teaching that believers are the present-day temple of God, the place of His worship and service. "Do you not know that you are a temple of God, and that the Spirit of God dwells in you" (1 Cor. 3:16)? Here in 1 Peter, the church is depicted as a spiritual house being built up by God Himself. Individual believers are the very stones by which this building is being constructed. Again we see that the Triune God alone gives growth to the church, yet the individual Christian is integral to that growth, being one of its living stones.

Peter began his picture of the temple with the emphasis on Christ Himself who is the "living stone" (v. 4). This "living stone," although rejected by His own people, was God's choice for the foundation of His building. The image of the Messiah as a rock rejected by the builders but chosen by God was an integral part of Christian teaching from the very earliest days.[1] Peter thus utilized the familiar imagery of the "rejected" rock and further fortified His insistence that Jesus the Messiah, was the cornerstone of the New Testament church by using several

Old Testament passages. The quotations in verse 6 (Isa. 28:16), verse 7 (Ps. 118:22), and verse 8 (Isa. 8:14) were used by the early church to confirm the role of the Messiah in the emerging New Testament community. The early Christians saw their faith as continuous with the people of God in the Old Testament. In the same instance, they also saw the uniqueness of the New Testament church. Here in the church God fully revealed His plan for the redemption of humankind through His very own Son.

If we take this image seriously, we must see ourselves as stones, integrally joined with those of the apostles and prophets themselves in the living temple of God. Here we see a stone with the name of Moses, this one with David's name, and over here are the stones representative of the apostles. Now joined to these stones, placed by the hand of Sovereign God Himself, is a stone on which your name is engraved. Nothing is more sobering nor challenging than this picture of the church.

The "corner stone" (1 Pet. 2:6) could be either the great foundational stone placed at the corner of the building or the topmost locking stone that gives strength to an arch. The possibility that one may stumble over this stone probably favors the suggestion that Peter had in mind the foundational stone. In either case, Christ is Himself the unique stone that gives life and meaning to the whole. Christ's function as the cornerstone means He is that stone that is precious and beloved by those who believe in Him. Yet He becomes the rock of stumbling for those who reject Him. They stumble because they are disobedient to the Word, and they chose not to accept Him as God's chosen stone. The refusal to accept God's choice stone thus will bring an appointed doom (v. 8). Notice that the consistent teaching of the New Testament is that persons belong to the church only by virtue of the new birth. They do not join the church: they are born into it.

In a passage with similar imagery Paul wrote: "If any man destroys the temple of God, God will destroy him, for the temple of God is holy, and that is what you are" (1 Cor. 3:17). Since the church is the temple of God on earth, it serves as the earthly place of worship and service to Holy God. For this reason, it must of necessity be pure. There can be nothing casual or light about our membership in this body.

A Holy Priesthood (v. 5,9)

The picture now shifts slightly as if we are viewing a beautiful diamond from another facet. Christians who were first pictured as stones in the temple are now seen as serving within the temple itself. If the temple exists for the service of God, it must be fitted with a priestly people to offer up sacrifices acceptable to Him.

In Exodus 19:5-6, the entire nation of Israel was called to a priestly function: "Now then, if you will indeed obey My voice and keep My covenant, then you shall be My own possession among all the peoples, for all the earth is Mine; and you shall be to Me a kingdom of priests and a holy nation." Notice that Israel was first called to radical obedience and holiness. When the conditions of the covenant were met, then Israel would be a special possession and a kingdom of priests (see Isa. 61:6). The responsibility of priesthood was a first priority.

The concept of a priestly nation made little headway where the levitical priesthood was highly honored. With the disappearance of an official priesthood in the early church, all chances of ambiguity were gone, and the theme of a priestly nation was directly applied to the church. Notice, for example, Revelation 1:6 ("He has made us to be a kingdom, priests to His God and Father") and Revelation 5:10 ("Thou hast made them to be a kingdom and priests to our God; and they will reign upon the earth").

What then are the functions of priests in the New Testament community? Peter gave us the first clue in 2:5, "to offer up spiritual sacrifices acceptable to God through Jesus Christ." The idea of a priest without a sacrifice is incongruous. The qualifying word, "spiritual," indicated that these sacrifices were intended to be nonmaterial in nature. The Old Testament writers paved the way for the understanding of the offering of nonmaterial sacrifices. The psalmist spoke of a sacrifice of thanksgiving (50:13-14) and that of a broken and contrite heart (51:17). In Psalm 141:2, prayer is viewed as an incense offering to God. The prophet Micah questioned whether God was delighted with thousands of rams and ten thousand rivers of oil or "to do justice, to love kindness,/And to walk humbly with your God" (Mic. 6:7-8).

Acceptable Sacrifices

Our Own Bodies

What then are acceptable New Testament sacrifices? What is the nature of our priestly task? I think we should start with the most basic sacrifice we have to offer—our own bodies. Paul wrote, "I urge you therefore, brethren, by the mercies of God, to present your bodies a living and holy sacrifice, acceptable to God, which is your spiritual service of worship" (Rom. 12:1). We inaugurate our priestly ministry by the offering of ourselves, our very bodies. We must give to "bodies" its full earthly meaning. We have nothing else to give God other than these earthly bodies our spirit calls home. It is here in the context of our physical bodies that our spiritual gifts operate. Paul pointedly charged the Corinthians, "You have been bought with a price: therefore glorify God in your body" (1 Cor. 6:20). We will never fulfill our priestly duties until we present our bodies as sacrifices acceptable to God.

This sacrifice implies our sexual and moral purity as 1 Corinthians 6:19-20 makes clear. It involves ministry and service that is sacrificial in nature. We rarely see sacrifice in the American church today. We often learn more about sacrifice by viewing the Olympics than we do by watching the church in action. We hear the stories of athletes who give up home and childhood for an Olympic medal. We hear examples of discipline and training that stagger the imagination. As we watch the best perform at their sport, we witness the results of sacrifice. If the church is going to make any significant impact on our world today, we must present our bodies as living sacrifices. We must train and prepare and function with discipline that befits our high calling.

Our Ministry

We should note that in Romans 15:16, Paul spoke of his ministry to the Gentiles as an offering sanctified by the Spirit. Further, we should not fail to notice that when Paul placed the Gentiles on the altar before God, he was presenting the results of his personal soul-winning. We can hardly claim to be priests if we are not personally involved in sharing the gospel and leading persons to Christ. The privilege of placing another life on the altar is the high calling of the priest. As we function in ministry according to our individual gifts, we offer to God an acceptable sacrifice. Accordingly, the failure to participate in the life and ministry of the church is to ignore the responsibility of the priesthood of believers.

Our Good Deeds

Good deeds are a third area of sacrifice mentioned in the New Testament. In Hebrews we read: "Do not neglect doing good and sharing; for with such sacrifices God is pleased" (Heb. 13:16). While good deeds cannot earn salvation, they become our priestly responsibility once we are saved. We place the labor of our hands on the altar before sovereign God.

Our Worship and Stewardship

Worship and stewardship are viewed as acceptable sacrifices by various New Testament writers. Paul, in thanking the Philippians for their financial support of his ministry, called their offering "a fragrant aroma, an acceptable sacrifice, well-pleasing to God" (Phil. 4:18). The writer of Hebrews encouraged his readers: "Through Him then, let us continually offer up a sacrifice of praise to God, that is, the fruit of lips that give thanks to His name" (Heb. 13:15). Growing churches are those with exciting worship services where the members offer a sacrifice of praise to God. The members come with eager anticipation to see God's hand at work. We cannot claim to be functioning as priests unless we are regularly offering up the sacrifice of worship through our attendance, praise, and stewardship. The Old Testament sacrificial system was built on the principle of offering our purest and our best. How can we as priests of a new and living temple act as if the standard has been lowered? Yet many believers attend worship when it is convenient. Statistics tell us that only about 20 percent of church members, those who claim to be priests, are faithful stewards. The priesthood of believers raises the stewardship of our money to the highest possible level. When we place our tithes and our offerings in the plate, we place it as a holy sacrifice before the living God in whose temple we serve.

Notice that Peter's emphasis is on the *function* of priesthood rather than on the *status* or *privilege* of priesthood. It is true that the concept of the priesthood of believers involves exhilarating privilege. We can know that our faith in Jesus Christ, not the intercession of another person, is that which justifies us before God. We can be assured that "we have boldness and confident access through faith in Him" (Eph. 3:12) at every juncture of our growing relationship with God.

Yet we must avoid the temptation to haul out the banner of "priesthood of believers" as if it were a "wild card" emphasizing only its privileges without due concern for its responsibilities. We're in danger of such behavior when we use it to boast of privilege, rather than as a willing commitment to offer up acceptable sacrifices. We're in danger of doing so when we insist on our right to do or act or believe as we please without due concern for the body of Christ. Let's commit ourselves to faithful exercise of the priestly duties rather than simply a selfish assertion of privilege.

In recent years the issue of the priesthood of believers and the role of the pastor have been held in opposition by some as if they are mutually exclusive ideas. This has led to a misunderstanding of both doctrines. All believers are priests and all are gifted; but that does not negate the fact that some persons are called to leadership functions. Neither pastoral leadership nor priestly service is an issue of authority. Both are matters of responsibility and function. In Hebrews 13:15-17 where two priestly sacrifices are mentioned (worship and good deeds) there is also an injunction: "Obey your leaders, and submit to them; for they keep watch over your souls, as those who will give an account. Let them do this with joy and not with grief, for this would be unprofitable for you." It is unfortunate that these two doctrines have ever been treated as being mutually exclusive. They are complimentary ideas.

People for God's Own Possession (vv. 9-12)

Finally Peter declared that we must be a holy people because God Himself desires to possess us! Look at these titles for the people of God: "You are a chosen race, a royal priesthood, a holy nation, a people for God's own possession" (v. 9). Notice that the emphasis in this verse is on our corporate identity. Even our priesthood is a corporate responsibility. We exercise our priestly functions in the corporate existence of the church. Thus it is not an individualistic idea, as if I can be a priest in and of myself. Consequently, as priests in the church, we are responsible to the community. The idea that priesthood means

I can do what I choose regardless of the needs of the brethren is a distortion. The suggestion that priesthood means I can worship God without due regard to the fellowship of the church is equally wrong. The suggestion that my priesthood frees me to interpret Scripture to please myself is utter nonsense. It would render the Holy Scriptures open to our every whim of interpretation. We as a priestly people are responsible to one another.

The priesthood of believers is primarily a corporate concept rather than an individual and private one. It certainly has meaningful personal consequences, as we have already seen, but its primary functions are corporate in nature. The biblical references to the priesthood of believers are plural, and this point is usually underlined with terms like "kingdom of priests," or "royal priesthood." An adequate understanding of this biblical truth should foster cooperation and unity as we work together as a nation "of priests."

We are corporately God's people because He purchased us with the blood of His Son. Now He desires to fully indwell us! Why does God desire to inhabit a people? The text is abundantly clear on this matter: "that you may proclaim the excellencies of Him who has called you out of darkness into His marvelous light" (v. 9). Once again we are confronted with a sobering fact. Holiness is demanded by our call to witness. We were nobodies, but He made us somebodies; our lives and our witness must reflect this truth. We must demonstrate to those in darkness the true nature of the light. Thus Peter gave another impassioned appeal for holiness. In verse 11, he warned us to abstain from fleshly lusts that wage war against the soul. If the standard of our behavior is excellence, there will be no opportunity for slander; instead, our transformed life-style will be an effective witness. The end result is that even the pagans will respond to the gospel as they see and hear our witness, and thus they will "glorify God in the day of visitation."

The call to be priests, to be a priestly nation, is one of the great truths of God's Word. It's time we cease to banter it around as merely a claim to privilege and begin to offer up spiritual sacrifices acceptable to God. Delos Miles says that one of the obstacles to church growth is that of paying lip service to the priesthood of believers.[2] Are you regularly laying acceptable sacrifices on the altar? Does your checkbook bear witness to the sacrifice of stewardship? Have you laid any "Gentiles" on the altar lately as the result of your personal soul-winning? How are your sacrifices of good deeds and worship? Ultimately, we must ask ourselves, "Have I placed my very body on the altar as living sacrifice? Priesthood of believers is no "wild" card containing unlimited privilege without responsibility. It is a biblical truth at the heart of the growing church.

Notes

1. Barnabas Lindas, *New Testament Apologetic* (London: Westminster, 1961), 169 *ff.*

2. Delos Miles, *Church Growth: A Mighty River* (Nashville: Broadman Press, 1981), 115.

10

Red Light—Green Light

"And if your brother sins, go and reprove him in private; if he listens to you, you have won your brother. "But if he does not listen to you, take one or two more with you, so that by the mouth of two or three witnesses every fact may be confirmed. "And if he refuses to listen to them, tell it to the church; and if he refuses to listen even to the church, let him be to you as a Gentile and a tax-gatherer. "Truly I say to you, whatever you shall bind on earth shall be bound in heaven; and whatever you loose on earth shall be loosed in heaven.

—Matthew 18:15-18

Red light, you're out.

"No way, I was stopped! You didn't see me moving!"

Do you remember the argument that ensued after this confrontation? I don't see children playing this game too frequently today. Maybe it's just as well since feelings were often hurt by what players perceived to be unfair judgments.

In case you're not familiar with this game, let me describe the way it was played. One child was chosen to be the "stoplight." The other children lined up at the other end of the playground and waited for the signal from the "stoplight." The "stoplight" turned his or her back and yelled "green light." The other players were free to run as far as they desired. The goal was to cross the finish line near the "stoplight" without being caught. The fun came in because the stoplight could turn red at any moment. When the "stoplight" turned "red," he or she would yell "red light" and turn quickly to catch any sign of movement. If players were caught moving, they were out of the game or, at least, sent back to the starting line.

Often when I bring up the topic of church discipline in a Bible study context, the attitude is that church discipline functions like a "red light." Its sole purpose is to catch the guilty and kick them out of the church. On some occasions I have had individuals ask me to invoke the "red light" on their spouses for suspected or known impropriety. "Maybe this will bring them to their senses." Such stern views of church discipline have led to a virtual neglect of this topic in the typical church. At the same time the church finds itself rendered virtually impotent by compromise and sins. Today it is often difficult to distinguish between the church and the secular world.

John Stott wrote: "The secular world is almost wholly unimpressed by the church today. There is widespread departure from Christian moral standards. So long as the church tolerates sin in itself and does not judge itself . . . and fails to manifest visibly the power of Jesus Christ to save from sin, it will never attract the world to Christ."[1]

How does this quotation by Stott make you feel? It makes me awfully uncomfortable, but I have to agree with its accuracy. The world really is not impressed. We are making virtually no inroads into pagan society. In a majority of denominations, baptisms are declining year after year. We're also becoming aware that society itself is becoming more and more secular. If anything, we are forced to admit that our secular culture is affecting the life-style and behavior of Christians more than we are changing the culture. George Gallup apparently agreed with Stott. He wrote: "Why does Christianity appear to be on the decline in some areas of the world? One reason is that Christianity is not lived—Christians are not living in such a way as to draw others to them."[2]

The church has opened itself to excessive complaints from our non-Christian neighbors. One can almost recite the litany of complaints:

"They're all a bunch of hypocrites. They go to church on Sunday, sure, but you should see their life-style the other days. They talk about family values, but they're just like us. They swap wives, they get divorces; then they just join another church and get active there. What's the difference?"

"Boy, those Christians! They talk about honesty, but the way they do business is shameful. I for one will never do business with another Christian."

"All those folks want is my money. They don't care about anyone—particularly me."

"They talk about love and fellowship. Yet all they do is fight! Some of them never speak to one another. The only way they start new churches is when they get mad enough to split!"

I know what you are thinking. There have always been critics of the church. People looking for hypocrites just want an excuse for their own life-style. They've got a bad attitude. It is true that the attitude of our critics is often wrong, but could it be that some of their criticisms may be painfully true? We cannot afford not to listen to these objections. If a spiritual awakening is to come to our nation, revival must begin in the house of God. We must honestly confess and repent of our sins and seek God's cleansing and healing. This is what the matter of church discipline is about.

Without question, church discipline has been used in a negative and abusive fashion. Sometimes church members have an unhealthy fascination with the exercise of discipline or the actual removal of a person from the church rolls. In the church we are brothers, not opponents. John White and Ken Blue in their excellent book on church discipline, *Healing the Wounded*, give several examples of non-biblical discipline.[3] In one instance, Saint Basil of Caesarea prescribed fifteen years of discipline for the sin of adultery. In those years the adulterer progressed from standing outside the door of the church to kneeling in the church while others stood. Finally, the person could join the regular service but could not take Communion. More recently there have been churches who, in the name of church discipline, publicly humiliated persons in a self-righteous manner. This is not in the spirit of biblical church discipline. The abuse of church discipline does not mean that we should totally ignore it. Recently, we have been made aware that surgery as a tool of healing has been abused on occasion. That does not mean we should not have surgery when it is necessary. Oftentimes it may be the only method to bring healing. Too much is at stake in the ministry of the church not to address the effect of sin on our witness and our fellowship. We must look at a biblical approach to constructive church discipline.

Context of Discipline

The Church Family

In Matthew 18:15-18, we should notice first that the context of discipline is the church family itself. Simply stated, discipline is a *family* issue. The church is called to be the pure bride of Christ. Therefore, we must recognize that our sinful condition affects the quality of the body life and effectiveness of our outreach. Recent nationwide religious scandals have vividly pointed to this issue of religious sin, but it is a matter that we must deal with constantly.

The Church Fellowship

Since we are *one* body in Christ, we must recognize the effect of sin on our fellowship. The body is such that when one rejoices, we all rejoice; and when one suffers, we all suffer together. We often interpret this last phrase in terms of death and bereavement. The church generally responds well when members suffer because of a death in their immediate family. There is an instant outpouring of empathy. We know what to do. We send flowers; we take in food; we offer to help with details and arrangements. But how do we respond when our brothers and sisters suffer as the result of sin in their lives? Notice that in verse 15 the introductory phrase is "If your brother sins."

The Neglect of Discipline

I think that we have neglected church discipline for three basic reasons. First, we do not place a sufficiently high premium on our church fellowship. Second, we do not fully appreciate the tragic results of our personal sins on the corporate life of the church. Third, we are not willing to pay the high cost of personal involvement.

The Result of Sin

What is the result of my personal sin on the life of the church family? In 1 Corinthians 5, in a passage dealing with church discipline, Paul wrote, "Do you not know that a little leaven leavens the whole lump of dough?" (v. 6). Leaven or yeast is such that even a small amount can penetrate an entire loaf of bread. Thus the sin of one individual penetrates and affects the life of the entire body. We have grown too casual about the result of sin in the life of the individual and the church. Sin destroys! It mangles! It disrupts fellowship! It weakens resistance! It dulls the conscience and debases the spiritual appetite! Thus sin makes us insensitive to the Spirit of God and unconcerned about fellowship. Sin always has a corporate effect. For example, if a husband is found embezzling funds at work, his sin has an impact on his entire family. So it is in the church: when one member sins, it has a leavening effect on the entire church family.

Here then is the context for understanding the need for church discipline. Sin compromises fellowship, it destroys *koinonia*, and thus, in the long run, it affects our ministry. Therefore, to appreciate the value of church discipline we must treasure church fellowship. We must value our fellowship so highly that when it is interrupted or lost, we persistently seek its restoration.

The Value of Fellowship

When we treasure something highly and then lose it, we seek it with a passion. Have you ever lost a piece of heirloom jewelry that has great sentimental value? The item may or may not have any particular economic value, but to you it is precious beyond any monetary measure. How do you react when you lose it? Do you say, "Oh, shucks, I lost my ring. I'll just have to buy another one." Not in my house! We begin a massive, house-altering search. The family is called to action. Couches and chairs and beds are moved and moved again. The trash is searched. We may find ourselves in the front yard on our knees at midnight with a flashlight in hand searching for this missing treasure. The search is not called off without our having expended every ounce of energy in our bodies. After all logical hope is lost, we continue to hope. We think of another possible location, and we dash there hoping against hope. Why? Because this heirloom is precious. It is irreplaceable.

When we come to the place that we consider our fellowship in the body of Christ to be a most precious possession, then we will seek to restore it at all costs. Only then will we understand the value and purpose of church discipline.

Purpose of Church Discipline

The key phrase for understanding the purpose of church discipline is found in Matthew 18:15: "You have won your brother." The desired end result of all church discipline is reconciliation and restoration. Our singular desire is to restore our brother and at the same time to strengthen the fellowship of the church for the sake of its mission. The church must be both pure and unified to be fully effective.

Church discipline rightly understood is ongoing training in the righteousness practiced by the church family in relationship to one another. It is not something that is done by a professional clergyman on behalf of the congregation. The intimate daily life in the church family requires correction, admonition, and encouragement. In 1 Thessalonians 5:14-16, Paul urged the brethren to "admonish the unruly, encourage the fainthearted, help the weak, be patient with all men. See that no one repays another with evil for evil, but always seek after that which is good for one another and for all men." This is the process of continual constructive church discipline.

How do you respond when someone in your Sunday school class behaves in an unruly manner and creates division in the class? Do you simply let it go, hoping it will die? Do you collar the pastor to resolve this problem since that's what "we pay him to do"? What is your personal response when you hear that a new Christian has fallen back into sinful ways? Do you exclaim, "I knew he wouldn't last! Just what I expected! If they keep going out into the highways and byways and dragging in all these sinners, it's bound to come to this. Good riddance is what I say." Or do you encourage the fainthearted with patience? You hear that someone has dropped out of choir because she got her feelings hurt when she didn't get a solo in the Christmas pageant. Do you simply think: *Then go! People that childish will get mad and leave over something else?* Or do you value fellowship so highly that you desire to patiently help those who are weak?

John White and Ken Blue indicated that there is actually a fourfold aim for church discipline:

1) Purity of the church; 2) Restoration of the sinner; 3) Freedom from sin; and 4) Reconciliation.

John and Ken also concluded that reconciliation is the primary aim and must be kept clearly in focus at all times. Issues such as purity and restoration are milestones on the way to putting an end to the alienation that separates an individual from God and from fellow church members.[4] Putting reconciliation first will keep us from being cruel, embarrassing a penitent sinner, or demanding that the church help us "get even." While we must desire reconciliation, we cannot overlook God's demand in both the Old and New Testaments that His people be pure. Purity is more than just a milestone on the way to reconciliation: it is the calling of God's people. Purity will, by definition, bring reconciliation.

Attitude for Discipline

The zeal for reconciliation demands a humble, loving attitude that prioritizes restoration. We can see this in the insistence in Matthew 18:15 that we first go alone to the person. Every precaution must be taken to ensure confidentiality and therefore pave the way for reconciliation. We can see this principle at work in Galatians 6:1-2: "Brethren, even if a man is caught in any trespass, you who are spiritual, restore such a one in a spirit of gentleness; each one looking to yourself, lest you too be tempted. Bear one another's burdens, and thus fulfill the law of Christ." Notice these key words and phrases: "restore," "spirit of gentleness," and "bear one another's burdens." The goal of discipline is restoration, and the attitude is gentleness. We remain gentle throughout the process because we realize that we stand only because of God's grace. We, ourselves, may be the next to be in need of the ministry of reconciliation. We would desire that those involved in our restoration would come to us with a sweet spirit of gentleness. This ministry requires that we be prepared to bear one another's burdens. It is costly. Yet it is commanded because it fulfills the law of Christ, which is the law of love.

Darrell Robinson pointed out that many Christians do not attempt restoration because they lack the willingness to bear one another's burdens. He wrote: "Why is restoration not attempted? Very simply, it is because we do not care enough to pay the price and risk involvement. There is a risk in becoming involved with people who have problems. We must love them enough to take the risk of being hurt ourselves in order to restore them."[5]

Steps to Discipline

Anytime I have mentioned the steps to church discipline, people are most interested in the final step. "Pastor, what do they have to do before we kick them out?" This is the "red light" syndrome I mentioned earlier. "I caught you moving; you're out of the game." I think that often the desire to understand the third step of church discipline comes from simple curiosity. Unfortunately, there is within most of us that peculiar desire to see the "hanging" or "follow the fire truck." We might be appalled at the hanging itself and look through our clasped fingers, but still we're drawn to the scene. Occasionally, folks come to me as a pastor inquiring about church discipline because they have been hurt by an unfaithful spouse or an unscrupulous businessman in the church. They want the church to make the guilty party pay. That attitude is indicative of the lack of understanding concerning the role of church discipline. Because there is such unanimous interest in this third step, I have chosen to look at it first, so we might properly focus on the first two.

The Third Step

The thrust of the entire New Testament on this matter of discipline is to avoid the final step: confrontation that may issue in withdrawing fellowship. The church and its members must literally exhaust every possible means to effect reconciliation before this final step of discipline is called for. We must exercise the seventy-times-seven rule of forgiveness in our intensity to see our brother or sister restored and reconciled (Matt. 18:22). In Luke's Gospel, the disciples were told to forgive the offending brother seven times a day. Both passages point to the long-suffering nature of forgiveness. In response to such demands, we like the early disciples cry out, "Increase our faith!" (Luke 17:5).

The reason for this caution is simple. This final step is an awesome and dramatic step. The severing of ties with a fellow member is not to be taken lightly. Matthew stated it as follows: "Let him be to you as a Gentile and a tax-gatherer" (18:17). Jesus used these two groups of persons in a proverbial way that His hearers would have quickly understood. A good Jew of Jesus' day did everything possible to avoid social intercourse with a Gentile or a tax-gatherer. Members being treated as Gentiles or tax-gatherers would be ostracized from the fellowship.

Some people associate the results of this final step with excommunication. Perhaps it would be more appropriate to refer to it as a quarantine. Individuals who refuse to respond to the repeated overtures for reconciliation from fellow believers have cut themselves off from all possibility of Christian fellowship. The desired result of this quarantine is to bring the unrepentant persons to their senses.

Two excellent examples of the application of this final step of church discipline can be found in the New Testament. The rare occurrence of disciplinary quarantine in the New Testament suggests it was not a frequent event and that it was treated with utmost seriousness. Indeed it was a final and bold attempt to confront sin when the first steps to reconciliation had been dutifully, patiently, and lovingly applied.

One prominent example of the third step of church discipline is found in 2 Thessalonians 3:12-15. The Thessalonian church had experienced explosive growth, so much so that Paul could say the story of their community had sounded forth even beyond the borders of Macedonia and Achaia (1 Thess. 1:8). Paul, however, was forced to leave Thessalonica earlier than he intended because of an uprising led by Jews jealous of Paul's success (Acts 17:5). Paul was duly concerned for the stability of the church in Thessalonica. Therefore, he seized the first opportunity to send Timothy to Thessalonica to strengthen the believers (1 Thess. 3:1-2). He also wrote two letters intended to complete and clarify some of his teaching.

Apparently there was some confusion in Thessalonica about the time of the second coming, and speculation seemed rampant. A few community members had proved themselves a hindrance to the stability of the community by their unruly behavior (*ataktos*). Some of these unruly folks were so convinced of the Lord's near return that they had quit working and would not support themselves or their families. They expected the hard-working community members to support them during their idleness. Obviously they had a great deal of free time, and they apparently had used this to spread dissension in the fellowship. Paul gave a one-sentence summary of their life-style: "We hear that some among you are leading an

undisciplined life, doing no work at all, but acting like busybo-
dies (2 Thess. 3:11).

Paul first exhorted the Thessalonians to change their present
life-styles (3:12). Second, he encouraged those who were
offended not to grow weary in doing good (v. 13). Our natural
tendency, when others seem to be getting by with the sin of
slothfulness, is to think we might as well relax ourselves: *Why
should I put out if nobody else is?* Third, Paul said that if a
repeat offender did not obey his instructions the people should
take special note of that person and "not associate with him"
(v. 14). Notice again that the desired result is that the brother
will feel the shame and be won back into the fellowship. We
see this clearly in the exhortation not to treat him as an enemy
but to admonish him as a brother. Paul was not suggesting
excommunication but quarantine with the desired end result
of restoration.

It is fascinating that one of the earliest examples of church
discipline had to do with persons who were spreading dissension in the church. Their negative, critical spirit had disrupted
the fellowship in Thessalonica and had thus affected its ministry. You should also notice that the refusal of a few persons to
work had proved to be a financial burden to some of the hard-
working members. The unruly brethren came to the church
family with open hands but without any apparent interest in
contributing to the life of the church. This critical spirit com-
bined with the financial drain could prove to be a severe hindrance to the effectiveness of the church's mission. Church
discipline is thus related to purity for the sake of effective
ministry. I would be so bold as to suggest that more damage
has been done to the fellowship and witness of the church by
a critical, divisive spirit and selfish attitude than has ever been
done by sexual sin.

A second example, however, deals with the matter of sexual
sin. In 1 Corinthians 5, we encounter a situation where a man
was living with his stepmother in an incestuous relationship.
The entire church apparently was aware of the sinful situation.
In fact, the text tells us that the individual was not only unrepentant but had himself been arrogant over the sin (1 Cor. 5:2).
Apparently, there were individuals in Corinth who believed
that their spirituality gave them a license to live above the

flesh. They were proud of this flagrant abuse of the flesh because, in their distorted thinking, it proved their spirituality.

Because of the arrogant and unrepentant behavior, Paul decided "to deliver such a one to Satan for the destruction of his flesh, that his spirit may be saved in the day of the Lord Jesus" (1 Cor. 5:5). While the terminology (deliver to Satan) is more striking, the desired result was the same as in the situation at Thessalonica: to save the spirit.

We don't appreciate the value of church discipline because we have not fully come to appreciate the importance of church membership and the value of our fellowship.

We have indicated already that the desire of church discipline at any level is to bring ultimate reconciliation and redemption. Probably this individual mentioned in 1 Corinthians 5 was restored to the fellowship of the church as recorded in 2 Corinthians 2:5-8. Paul indicated that the punishment inflicted by the majority was sufficient. They were to forgive and comfort him and reaffirm their love for him. If indeed these two passages are related, then even this final dramatic step of discipline had the desired effect of restoration.

Thus I would suggest that this last step of bringing the offending brother before the assembly must involve a sinful act in which he is (1) arrogant, (2) blatant, (3) unrepentant, and (4) its being broadly known in the church and in the community affects the fellowship and the witness of the church.

Notice that the final stage of church discipline is not to be understood as a divorce court or a place to resolve hurt feelings. The church is not a place to air our own personal interpretation of another individual's life-style. We should not just display our dirty laundry before the world or use the church to get back at those who have hurt us. It is not a place for the public confession of every private sin. Church discipline is too serious a matter to treat lightly. The public exposure of sin is to be called for only when every other attempt to bring reconciliation has been patiently, lovingly, and thoroughly explored. Then, and only then, does the church move to formally recognize that which has already occurred.

We should focus on ongoing discipline, so that this final step never becomes a necessity. Now let's look at the first two steps of church discipline.

The First Step

The first step in maintaining fellowship is that we go in private to the person who has sinned with the goal of restoration. Notice that we must go alone and go with the singular focus of restoration. Look at the beauty of this first step. If practiced faithfully, it would avoid the possibility of gossip. All too often when one is hurt, whether it is in a marriage or in a Sunday School class, the hurt is spread by telling others before attempting to resolve the hurt ourselves. The word spreads, people start choosing sides, and the chasm opens wider. I can't tell you how often I have seen a small and reconcilable marital issue end in divorce because both partners began telling their story before they truly sought personal reconciliation.

The first step in reconciliation is personal and private. Now some of you may be thinking that you need to get advice. Do not. Go alone! The publicity may itself hinder reconciliation. The individual may justifiably ask, "Who else knew you were coming to me?" When you confront the person, you may discover that the whole issue is a huge misunderstanding. How could you then undo the story if you had shared it with anyone else?

"Well, shouldn't I pray about it with someone first?" you might ask. Prayer can be the most subtle form of gossip in the evangelical community. The first priority is absolute confidentiality. Obey God and depend on Him in prayer. I believe that when this step is lovingly and patiently applied, healing will follow in most instances.

I had an opportunity to see personal confrontation bring reconciliation, although it was not strictly a one-on-one situation. I had led a young man to Christ who came from a very sinful past. He had spent many evenings at local bars drinking and brawling. When he discovered the power of God to forgive his sin, he responded with great joy. He joined the church and was baptized. Proudly, he brought his entire family to church week after week. They would sit on the front row. One Sunday he was not there. I didn't think much about it. I was a little more concerned when I noticed his absence the next Sunday.

After church on that Sunday, I noticed that one of the deacons had waited around until everyone had left. That should have made me suspicious since he was usually the first to dash home. He walked up and asked about the absence of "my convert."

"Do you know where he was last night?" he inquired.

"No," I responded. "Do you?"

"Yes, he was back at the bar again."

"How do you know?" I questioned, with a tinge of accusation in my voice. He never answered that. Then I asked if the deacon had attempted to visit our church member to restore him to the fellowship.

I went straight to the young man's home. When I walked in, he dropped his head in shame. He hadn't shaved in two weeks. We walked outside the house into a dried-out hog lot.

"Where have you been? What's wrong?"

He couldn't answer. He began to weep. "I've blown it. Can God ever forgive me?"

We knelt together in the red clay of that hog lot and wept. He had experienced forgiveness, and he was restored to God's family. That is church discipline in action.

The Second Step

If the first step has been faithfully followed and there is no reconciliation, God provides the opportunity to take two or three witnesses. The witnesses can help persuade the offender to repent and to be reconciled. The witnesses also ensure objectivity, safety, and fairness. Notice again that the small number of witnesses provides for confidentiality. The demand for two or three witnesses was a long-standing Jewish tradition. The ultimate concern is that the multiple testimony will provide a more convincing case to effect reconciliation.

Who should be chosen as the witnesses? The Bible doesn't specify this. They certainly must be mature and trustworthy believers who can keep a confidence. The witnesses themselves are brought to function as reconcilers, not to prove someone's case. They may be able to assist in the recommendation of restorative measures when repentance occurs. Again, we should bear in mind that there are to be no bounds to our forgiveness or our desire to bring reconciliation.

Notice the seriousness of church fellowship. In Matthew 18:18 we see the New Testament church exercising the authority of the keys. In this instance the binding and loosing refer to the withholding of fellowship or the restoration of fellowship because of the reconciliation that has occurred through church discipline.

Church is no game! We're not playing "Red Light—Green Light" with church members. We don't win just because we avoid detection. The mission of the church is vital. Heaven and hell are at stake. Our fellowship and our purity affect our witness. There is no place for apathy concerning impurity. At the same time, we cannot allow hurt feelings, petty misunderstandings, and unresolved hostilities to cripple the ministry of the church. Too much is at stake. We must find a place for balanced, biblical church discipline. Our primary goal must be the reclaiming and restoration of believers along with the maintenance of a pure witness to the world.

Notes

1. John Stott, *Confess Your Sins: The Way of Reconciliation* (Waco, Tex.: Word, 1974), 49.

2. George Gallup, "Worldwide Trends in Religion" (Speech given at the Biennial Meeting of the Lausanne Committee for World Evangelization, 22 January 1987), 17.

3. John White and Ken Blue, *Healing the Wounded* (Powers Grove, Ill.: InterVarsity Press, 1985), 45-56. For those interested in a major, thorough discussion of church discipline, this book will prove to be an excellent resource.

4. Ibid.

5. Darrell W. Robinson, *Total Church Life* (Nashville: Broadman Press, 1985), 61.

Choosing Up Sides

For through the grace given to me I say to every man among you not to think more highly of himself than he ought to think; but to think so as to have sound judgment, as God has allotted to each a measure of faith. For just as we have many members in one body and all the members do not have the same function, so we, who are many, are one body in Christ, and individually members one of another. And since we have gifts that differ according to the grace given to us, let each exercise them accordingly: if prophecy, according to the proportion of his faith; if service, in his serving; or he who teaches, in his teaching; or he who exhorts, in his exhortation; he who gives, with liberality; he who leads, with diligence; he who shows mercy, with cheerfulness.

—Romans 12:3-8

One of the most painful experiences of childhood was often "choosing up sides." This ritual preceeded many team events. I remember it most clearly in connection with summer baseball games. Usually the two best athletes were asked to choose their teams. Someone would determine who would get first choice, and then the process would commence. The person selecting first generally would choose his best friend and the same would occur with his opponent.

Then the strategy would begin in earnest. The two friends would confer concerning the next choice. Sometimes, their whispers would be painfully loud. "No, not Ken; he couldn't catch a fly ball with a bucket. Let's take Charlie; he's a good batter and runs well." In most instances the first four or five selections went quickly. Everyone knew who the best atheletes were! As each player was chosen, he took his position behind the captain.

The pace of the choosing slowed down; the whispers grew louder as more team members added their two-cents worth. But most painfully, the talent pool grew smaller and smaller. If you were among those remaining few, you knew all eyes were trained on you. Your greatest fear was that you would be chosen dead last! What a put-down! I can even remember times that there would be a deal struck in order to get everybody on a team. "Listen, you take Ken, and I'll take the other two." That was inspiring. Nothing like being wanted and needed. So I wasn't the best fielder. I could do other things well. I could hit and run. Surely I could help the team somewhere.

The good news about the use of spiritual gifts in the life of the church is that no one is chosen last. In fact, God has placed all the members in the church with just the gifts as He Himself chose.

Although there are a variety of spiritual gifts, all are equally important in the economy of the New Testament church. But how many gifts are there? Do all the gifts still exist? Do I have any? How can I know what my gifts are? Questions like these and others concerning gifts have grown in frequency today. Many churches fail to address this question, and, consequently, they neglect some of the greatest and most affirming truths of the Word of God.

This chapter will be much too brief to answer all the questions you might have on spiritual gifts. I will not attempt in this book to address all the issues raised concerning spiritual gifts, nor will I attempt to look at all the gift passages. I have addressed this issue in greater detail in *Spiritual Gifts: Empowering the New Testament Church*, published by Broadman. That book treats the major gift passages in their historical and theological context.[1]

In this chapter we will look at the five important principles of gifted ministry. These principles could be developed from either 1 Corinthians 12 or Romans 12. I have selected Romans 12 because it provides a synthesis of Paul's teaching. In the Corinthian letter, Paul had to put out numerous brush fires due to inadequate understanding before he could share his own conviction about the operation of spiritual gifts.

Principle of Universal Giftedness

To find our first principle we need to look at Romans 12:6 and discover the foundational truth of this entire passage: "Since we have gifts that differ according to the grace given to us." This sentence begins with a participle phrase that states Paul's basic assumption, namely, all Christians are gifted. Throughout his letters, Paul hammered away at this central truth. In 1 Corinthians 12:6, he declared that the same God "works *all* things in *all* persons" (author's italics). In verse 7 of that same chapter, Paul repeated this truth with an even more personal emphasis: "But to *each one* is given the manifestation of the Spirit for the common good" (author's italics). In Romans and 1 Corinthians Paul utilized the picture of a functioning human body to puncture the false notion that only a few spiritually elite persons are gifted. This idea still circulates today in some circles, but we need only to read the text to understand how blatantly false it is.

There are two obvious implications of this first principle. First, there are no *spectators* in the body of Christ. You were saved and gifted by God to serve! Second, all the members of the body must work together if the church is to operate at full effectiveness. You are important to the work of the church!

You may be wondering what sort of abilities are covered by the term "spiritual gifts." We often turn to one of the gift lists to discover the answer to this question. There are four lists: 1 Corinthians 12:8-10; 12:28-29; Romans 12:6-8; and Ephesians 4:11. These lists are representative, not exhaustive. They were intended only to illustrate the sort of abilities and activities one might call "spiritual gifts." There is no value in combining the various lists and identifying twelve or sixteen gifts. God is a God of infinite creativity, and He is still creating gifts for the church today as it faces new challenges and tasks.

The gift lists are distinctively different, and each serves a different purpose. The first list in 1 Corinthians 12:8-10 incorporates the gifts highly valued by a group of folks in Corinth that I like to identify as the "spirituals." These individuals sought gifts for their sign value. They believed that certain miraculous gifts were signs of God's favor and proved their advanced spirituality. Therefore, it should not surprise us that the first gift list primarily included gifts that are "miraculous in nature" and that would be prominent in the gathered assembly (1 Cor. 12:8-10).

In the second list (12:28-29), Paul intentionally chose certain gifts in order to expand the Corinthians' understanding of the types of abilities that were given by God for ministry. You will notice that he included several of the gifts from the first list, but he sandwiched them between leadership abilities (apostles, prophets, and teachers) and service abilities (helps and administrations). Paul literally stretched the Corinthian understanding of spiritual gifts by demonstrating that service abilities and leadership functions are also gifts of the Spirit of God. All subsequent gift lists emphasize leadership functions and service gifts as well. These were the gifts most useful in the life of the church.

As you look at the gift list in Romans 12:6-8, you will notice that it lists only a few gifts. Yet the list is intentionally broad to illustrate that all gifts given for service are spiritual gifts. We have the expected gifts, such as prophecy and teaching, but they are joined by exhortation, giving, leading, and showing mercy.

Because we have failed to address this matter of spiritual gifts in the church, we have left them enveloped in a cloud of mystery. Most persons whom I have talked to who have accepted Christ as Savior, having thus been empowered by God's Spirit, do not wake up the next morning with a new gift or ability to serve God. Frankly, as a pastor, if I were approached by a new believer who wanted to jump right in and teach in our church on the basis that they had just received a gift for teaching, I would be more than a little cautious. In fact, most pastors would want to spend time with these persons, making sure they attended training sessions and had some understanding of the doctrinal stance of the church. The fact that someone is gifted for service does not mean that they shouldn't seek training or develop their gifts. You should notice that Ephesians 4:11-12 indicates that the pastor/teacher must equip the saints for the work of service. Gifts can and should be developed through the ongoing equipping ministry of the church.

If the way spiritual gifts work is not all that mysterious, then how do I discover my giftedness? How many gifts exist? I think that any ability that enables one to serve the church can rightly be called a spiritual gift when it meets the following criteria.

Criteria for Spiritual Gifts

1. *It must be recognized and acknowledged as a gracious gift of the sovereign God.*—When persons accept Christ, they receive the Spirit of God that enables them to understand spiritual truths (1 Cor. 2:6-16). This is why individuals can only truly understand and love the Bible after they are saved. They are transferred from the kingdom of darkness to the kingdom of light. The Holy Spirit is imparted to teach them concerning all spiritual truths. Therefore, rather than receiving new abilities not previously possessed, often new believers begin to see their abilities in a new light. They are now able to recognize "the things freely given to us by God" (1 Cor. 2:12). For the first time, believers can truly comprehend that everything they have ever possessed, including talents and abilities, is a gift from God. Paul asked the Corinthian believers a very pointed question: "What do you have that you did not receive?" (1 Cor. 4:7).

This is not to suggest that the sovereign God does not, or cannot, give uniquely new gifts to an individual or the church as they are needed. Often a young pastor, in his first church, discovers that his role as pastor requires an administrative gift that he has not previously demonstrated. He may diligently seek this gift from the Lord. The fact that gifts are *given* does not negate the fact that the Scriptures encourage us to *seek* those that edify the church. The pastor in our example will probably also consult with mature pastors for guidance in fulfilling his administrative duties. He may read suggested books or articles on church administration as he continues to seek this gift in prayer. It may well be that the administrative gift will soon become this young pastor's strongest gift. To seek a gift from God does not mean we should not ourselves seek to develop it, any more than praying for a friend's salvation means we should not actively witness to the friend. Thus, even in the area of gifts, there is cooperation between a sovereign God who gives as He chooses and the freedom of the individual who seeks and responds to God.

2. *Once our talents and abilities have been discerned to be gracious gifts from God, they must then be surrendered to His lordship.*—It is in this point of surrender that the gifts are fully

empowered by God's Spirit. This is a principle that most of us have learned in the Christian life but have seldom applied to the doctrine of spiritual gifts. Simply stated: it is in the surrender of ourselves that we experience the full empowering of God's Spirit.

3. *Our gifts must be used for the service of the body of Christ.*—The gifts are given by God to equip His body for service; therefore, when they are surrendered, they are returned to God for service in His body. There is a real sense of stewardship concerning the use of our gifts for service to others.

Principle of Sober Evaluation

There are two inherent problems with spiritual gifts. The first is that of overevaluation, which creates spiritual arrogance. Overevaluation comes when people see their gifts as a sign of their spiritual maturity. This apparently was a problem in Corinth. In answering the Corinthians' inquiry concerning gifts, Paul gave an important corrective in his use of terminology. The Corinthians asked concerning the *pneumatika* (12:1). That word comes from the Greek root *pneuma,* which means "spirit." They believed that the gifts were manifestations of the Spirit. They also believed that the possession of certain gifts proved one to be spiritually elite. This same idea is found today in the suggestion that speaking in tongues is proof that one is filled with the Spirit. Paul responded to their question with the word *charismata,* (v. 4) which comes from the root word *charis,* meaning grace. Here's the point: *gifts tell us nothing about the possessor but everything about the Giver.* God is gracious to gift His church for every task. Since all gifts are expressions of the grace of God, why should anyone boast or become arrogant?

The second problem is that of under evaluation. Frequently, this problem is more prevalent in the church than overevaluation. This individual declares, "Woe is me; I'm not gifted. There is nothing I can do in the church." This is the Eeyore mentality. You'll recall that Eeyore is the flop-eared donkey in *Winnie the Pooh* that mopes around, tail between his legs, thinking he is of no worth. Under evaluation is equally sinful because it denies the Word of God (all are gifted), and it deprives the church. Paul required that we think "so as to have sound judgment, as God has allotted to each a measure of faith" (12:3). This unusual phrase "measure of faith" is essentially the same as "spiritual gift." Any Christian who fails to utilize his or her gift in service to the church deprives the body of Christ and is guilty of bad stewardship.

Unity in Diversity (vv. 4-5)

In our diversity we experience unity. We can see this clearly when we look at the human body. Each of our five fingers operate somewhat differently. They must do so to function as a hand. Our eyes have a different function than the ear or the foot. Each must do their task well if the body is to function as a unified whole. This was precisely the point Paul intended to make when he used the human body to illustrate the working of spiritual gifts in 1 Corinthians 12:12-16. This suggests two equally important truths: no one individual can do it all, and everyone must do their assigned tasks.

Let me illustrate these two points with two different sports stories from my own past. I played linebacker for Wake Forest University. In practice we constantly drilled on the linebacker's responsibilities. One of the instructions repeated over and over again was "play your own position." It's always tempting to think that you can outsmart the opposition and make an outstanding play. The linebacker keys off of the offensive lineman in front of him. If this guy pass blocks, you retreat to your assigned passing zone. If he fires out at you, you fill the hole. If he pulls down the line, you go with him. It was this last key that was often hard to obey. When the guard pulls, it leaves this huge gap in the line. Being agile and quick, the linebacker often thinks, *I'll just shoot through that hole and tackle the quarterback before the play can develop.*

One fall afternoon in Bowman Grey Stadium, the temptation of that gaping hole in the line became much too strong. The guard pulled, and I zipped through the line and made the tackle behind the lines. The fans went wild. I listened to be sure they gave me credit over the public address system for the tackle. This went on play after play. I was having a great time in the opponent's backfield. I was a veritable one-man team. I was all over the field playing everybody's position. We came back out for the second half, and I braced myself for more of the same. On the first series of plays, the guard in front of me pulled out, and I shot the gap, hungry to tackle the opposing quarterback. All of a sudden I was trap blocked from the opposite side. I never saw the guy coming! I looked up in time to watch the runner scamper through my hole for a touchdown. We were beaten that afternoon, and much of the credit goes to a linebacker who thought he could do it all himself.

The second story originates in England. When I arrived for graduate studies in England, I decided to find a new team sport in which to participate. Because of my background in football, some of my English friends took me to a rugby practice. I thought football was bad enough, but the idea of playing football without pads appealed to me even less. I watched a cricket match and decided it was too slow. Then one day I discovered rowing. I was walking by the Cam River when this sleek eight passed by me: *Now there's a sport for me.* It looked so peaceful as the boat glided effortlessly along the beautiful tree-lined Cam. Here was a sport with scenery: majestic trees, lovely ladies, colorful ducks, and immaculate English gardens that backed up to the river. I was hooked. When I learned that all the ducks belonged to the queen, I was convinced rowing was for me. After all, I would be among royalty.

After only a few practices I discovered that looks can deceive. You talk about painful! Rowing is a little like running a marathon and doing sit-ups at the same time. I'm no quitter, so I decided to stick it out. After several practices, I developed an intense distaste for one of the individuals in our boat. It wasn't that I disliked him personally, it was his job. He was the cox. This guy stood about five feet, six inches, and weighed about eighty-five pounds soaking wet. But the problem was that he didn't do anything. He just sat in the rear of the boat and steered while we provided all the manpower. Even more frustrating was that he often chastised us for not working hard enough. I often thought: *What use is this guy? If we could just dump him, we'd be eighty-five pounds lighter, and my work would be easier.*

Finally, the day of the race came. The annual regatta in Cambridge is unique to say the least. The river is too narrow for two boats to race side by side. Therefore, the eighteen or so boats in each heat are lined up, one in front of the other. The rules are relatively simple. Contestants must catch and bump the boat immediately in front of them before the boat behind catches them. Sounds simple, but you must take into account that the oarsmen sit facing the rear. The only person facing frontwards is—you guessed it—the cox. To help the oarsmen to know when the boat was close enough to make a bump, there was a bank party giving signals. The signals were simple, like a whistle or bell. The signals worked well in practice, but on the day of the race everything changed. All eighteen boats devised their own set of signals. Mix all the bells and whistles with thousands of screaming spectators, and you will have an accurate picture of the pandemonium that reigns on race day.

One day, while watching one of the heats prior to our own, I discovered why the the cox was needed. The boat in question was preparing for a bump. They had been moving well, and they were in the final powerful strokes to assure that they had sufficient overlap. The cox was counting out the strokes to ensure perfect timing. Inexplicably, the cox turned to glimpse the boat behind him. In so doing he slightly turned the boat to the left and simultaneously failed to notice that the river took a sharp right turn. There was a bump all right, but it was with a stump on the riverbank. Who would ever have thought that the cox's task was all that important. But when he neglected his task, the efforts of the others were affected.

There are no persons chosen last when it comes to spiritual gifts. All are equally important even though they have different functions.

Interdependence

Paul declared with awe that we are "members one of another." One of the greatest truths about spiritual gifts is that they make us interdependent. I often hear people and churches declare their independence, "I don't need anyone else to live the Christian life." Nothing could be further from the truth. The fact that no one has all the gifts renders us dependent on one another. I need your gifts to complement mine, and you need mine in the same way. I need your gifts not only to make mine complete, but I depend on your gifts because they minister to me. As believers we are so much a part of one another that when one rejoices, all rejoice, and when one suffers, all suffer.

A stronger reaffirmation of the local church could hardly be found. God exercises His sovereignty as He Himself places the members in the body as He chooses. A body member separated from the body has neither purpose nor vitality. We might watch a gifted pianist and react by saying, "He has gifted hands." Those gifted hands severed from the body become lifeless and useless. We must ask whether this truth accounts for the harrowing downfall of some of the "gifted" televangelists who felt they could go it alone without being accountable to the church.

Common Good

Spiritual gifts are given with a singular goal—to edify the body of Christ. The spirituals in Corinth believed them to have sign value. They thought that certain of the gifts proved that they were spiritually elite. Paul categorically stated that the gifts have no value in the body of Christ unless they edify other believers. Even a cursory reading of 1 Corinthians 14 indicates that Paul desired for the Corinthians to seek primarily those gifts that would edify the church (1 Cor. 14:12). He also instructed them on how to use any gifts in an edifying fashion.

Conclusions

There are several obvious and challenging conclusions. First, we are co-workers with God and gifted to do whatever He calls us to do. Second, no task is mundane or insignificant. Whether it is changing diapers in preschool, ushering, or working in the parking lot, if we properly understand our labor in the perspective of Christ's body, we will see that eternity itself is at stake. No task is insignificant to the mission of the church. God has designed the body and placed each person in it just as He has chosen. Third, we are led to the inevitable conclusion that no person is unimportant. There are a number of books dealing with self-image on the market today. Nothing can build self-worth as effectively as the realization that we are an integral part of God's eternal purpose in the church. God Himself has chosen us and gifted us for service. Finally, we can see that no task is too great for the church. If the God who gives the task also equips the church, there is no reason we cannot be effective in His service.

One of the dilemmas often encountered in the "choosing up" of sides was that a captain would choose his team based on friendship, not ability. This strategy almost invariably proved to be disastrous. In other instances, the captain would choose the team without due consideration for the actual needs of the team and the abilities of those in the talent pool. Thus, on some occasions the captain would end up with a number of good hitters but rather inept fielders. Here again the selection process proved to be the team's undoing.

The good news about the giftedness of the church is that God placed the members in the body just as He chose. No one will be selected last or be grouped together and bartered for. God is able to provide every ability necessary for the proper functioning of His body. He knows our ability for service because He gifted us through the work of His Spirit, and He wants us to participate where we are best qualified for meaningful service.

Join the team. You've just been selected by God Himself!

Notes

1. If you are interested in discovering your Spiritual gifts, you might want to read the following: Gerry Peak, *Study Guide to Spiritual Gifts: Empowering the New Testament Church* (Nashville: Broadman Press, 1990); *Discovering Your Spiritual Gifts*, Equipping Center, Baptist Book Store catalogue #7678-71. Call 1-800-458-BSSB.

12

King of the Mountain

But we request of you, brethren, that you appreciate those who diligently labor among you, and have charge over you in the Lord and give you instruction, and that you esteem them very highly in love because of their work. Live in peace with one another. And we urge you, brethren, admonish the unruly, encourage the fainthearted, help the weak, be patient with all men.

—1 Thessalonians 5:12-14

I'm king of the mountain." This shout usually heralded the beginning of one of my favorite childhood games. The playing field was simple. A good-sized dirt pile was all that was required. Dirt piles were easily found in neighborhoods where new construction was taking place. The contractor created a sufficiently high mound of dirt while excavating for the basement or the foundation of the house.

The rules were even simpler than the playing field. One person claimed the top of the mound and declared himself to be the king of that mountain. The other participants then attempted to dethrone him. Usually the attempts were frontal attacks as child after child rushed the hill and tried to shove the king aside. If another participant succeeded in dethroning the "king," he, in turn, became king, and the game continued. Sometimes a particularly strong or agile youth could manage to stay up for quite a long period of time.

If the reigning king were not dethroned quickly enough to suit all the players, we would sometimes develop a strategy to "get him." "OK, you guys rush from the front and get his attention, and I will grab his legs from behind. If I can't pull him down by myself, we'll get him together." Usually there were several kings before the game ended. Everyone finally got tired of pushing, shoving, and yanking, and just quit. By this time, considerable damage had been done to the hill, our clothes, and our egos. We never could decide that there was a clear-cut winner. Almost everyone spent a few minutes on top, but they were often rather fleeting and usually unsatisfying as king after king bit the dust.

Tragically, I hear of churches where it sounds like they're playing "king of the mountain" when it comes to church leadership. A constant struggle takes place between pastor, deacons, and/or elders, and other laity to see who is king of the mountain. If the struggle becomes intense, coalitions can be formed to dethrone the ruling king. Often the winner is determined only by the fact that he or she remains standing after the struggle. Here too, "ruling the mountain" brings little satisfaction because you are always fighting to retain your authority. In many cases, both the playing field and the participants show the effects of the battle. After the dust finally settles, we realize that no one won, and everyone is the loser. Most participants just get tired of the game and quit. The church and its witness suffer irreparable damage from such leadership games.

The issue we are addressing is that of leadership. If we look at two of the earliest passages dealing with community ministry (Gal. 6:1-6; 1 Thess. 5:12-14), we find two consistent themes. First, every member of the body is responsible for ministry within the fellowship. Christians are saved to serve. This reminds us of the responsibility that comes with the priesthood of believers. Second, there are, in every community, those who are called to exercise leadership functions. These are not mutually exclusive ideas but rather complementary ones. They demonstrate that there is a God-ordained structure for the mutual benefit of everyone in the community. We'll focus our attention on 1 Thessalonians 5:12-14.

Proper Relationships for Leadership

Paul began this section on leadership by addressing the brethren concerning their relationship to those who were in leadership positions. "We request of you, brethren, that you *appreciate* those who diligently labor among you, and have charge over you in the Lord and give you instruction, and that you *esteem* them very *highly in love* because of their work. Live in *peace with one another*" (1 Thess. 5:12-13, author's italics). Possibly, some tension existed in Thessalonica between leaders and laity. Paul was forced to leave Thessalonica so quickly that it may not have been entirely clear who were the leaders. Several individuals may have been pulling in different directions. Some community members were tired of the power struggle and were tempted to ignore all prophetic utterances. Unfortunately, we often find a similar distance or wall of separation between leaders and the laity in churches today.[1]

George Gallup once illustrated this apparent hostility with a story of a mother and a son arguing at the breakfast table on Sunday morning about whether the son was going to church or not. Finally the son said, "I can think of two good reasons why I *shouldn't* go to church. First of all, I don't like any of the people there very much, and secondly, none of the people there like me."

The mother answered him right back, saying, "Well, I can think of two good reasons why you *should* go to church. First of all, you're forty-five years old, and, secondly, they pay you to be the rector of the church!"[2]

When we hear of friction between pastor and laity, we must remind ourselves of the significance of the mission of the church. We are called out and commissioned by God to fulfill the Great Commission. We are empowered to deal with issues affecting eternity. Because of the work of the church, there must be nothing that stands in the way of the proper functioning of the body. Our priority must be to develop and nurture a loving relationship between the people and those in leadership positions. We must keep the task of the church clearly in focus.

How often have you known of the work of a local church being hindered because of dissension between the people and the leadership? All too often I encounter a suspicious attitude that manifests itself in a "we-them" mentality. We hear it in statements like: "*We've* got to watch that preacher; *he* likes to spend *our* money," or, "Who does *he* think he is, trying to run *our* church," or conversely, "*I'll* never get these people to do anything; *they're* so set in their ways." Sometimes I detect this thinking in the harsh jokes preachers tell about deacons or those that laypersons tell about preachers.

It is true that many pastors are made to feel like itinerants, never being accepted as part of the church or the community. On the other hand, pastors have often caused or added to this feeling by giving every appearance of being transitory. All too often when we arrive, we're already contemplating our next step up the ladder to a larger church or a bigger community. Whatever the historical causes or the present reasons for this "we-them" mentality, we must banish it for the sake of our work. We must remove it from our vocabulary, our thought processes, and even our subtle but stinging jokes.

Only through mutual esteem and love can we "live in peace with one another" (v. 13). The brethren must appreciate and esteem highly in love those who are called by God into a leadership function. Yet this love and appreciation must be earned through the efforts of our labors together. I am convinced that peace in the church body as a whole begins with a loving relationship between pastor and people.

Appropriate Functions

In the passage from Thessalonians 5, a threefold task is given to the leader. In the Greek there are three present participles governed by a single article that indicates we are looking at one group of persons who accomplish three specified tasks. This passage forms somewhat of an early job description for the leaders of the church. I think you'll discover that this three-fold function is not altered throughout the New Testament.

Labor Among

The leader first is called to care for the church by working hard in their midst. "Labor among" points to the hard work entailed in the task of pastoral leadership. When Paul wrote Timothy concerning his pastoral ministry, he encouraged Timothy concerning both his physical and spiritual fitness. The labor of pastoral ministry is demanding physically, emotionally, and spiritually. While I know this to be true, both as the son of a pastor and as a pastor myself, I find many laypersons who believe that pastors are lazy. I'm quite sure that much of this misunderstanding comes from a failure on the part of church members to understand all that is involved in the pastoral work. Most folks see only that which is visible, the Sunday morning or Sunday night preaching appearance. It would be both instructive and valuable for laypersons to develop an understanding of what the pastor's weekly schedule is like. The best way I know to accomplish this is to spend time with your pastor and ask questions about his work that communicate interest and support. Again, we must ban the stereotypical preacher jokes suggesting that the pastor only works a couple of hours a week. Unfortunately, people take our jokes seriously.

Here, I must say a word to pastors. We are a discredit to our profession, and we destroy the trust relationship with our people when we are poor stewards of our time. Because of the nature of our work, we have every opportunity to be lazy if we so desire. We too must remember the eternal nature of our work and to whom we are ultimately accountable.

I believe that the functional element of pastoral care is present in this phrase "labor among." Leaders are not just called to work hard, but to work hard *among* their people. They must provide pastoral caring and prove to be an example of ministry for others in the congregation.

Have Charge Over

The function described by the Greek *proistēmi* is that of oversight, leadership, and protection. This term describes the administrative role of the pastor. The Greek term *proistēmi* is used in the gift list in Romans 12:8 to describe the person gifted in exhortation. A feminine form of the word is used in Romans 16:2 to describe Phoebe, who was a "helper of many." Outside our present context and the two occurrences in Romans, this term is found elsewhere in the New Testament only in the Pastoral Letters. On three occasions it is used in the Pastoral Letters to describe the requirement that the overseer and the deacons must *lead* their own households (1 Tim. 3:4,5, 12). The obvious implication is that those who are entrusted to lead the church must be able to lead at home. Pastors must demonstrate their leadership in the smaller context of their homes before being entrusted with the greater responsibility of the church. In 1 Timothy 5:17, *proistēmi* is used in conjunction with the term *elder*: "Let the elders who rule well be considered worthy of double honor, especially those who work hard at preaching and teaching."[3] Although a different Greek term is used in Hebrews 13:17, we have a parallel passage. The writer commanded his readers, "Obey your leaders and submit to them, for they keep watch over your souls, as those who will give an account." The pastor is accountable before God for the spiritual oversight of the church.

Numerous studies have demonstrated that growing churches are those that give their pastors the responsibility and freedom to oversee the mission of the church. The New Testament evidence indicates that this is a God-given responsibility of the pastor. Yet there is both confusion and disagreement on the issue of pastoral leadership today. The task of leadership not only gives great opportunity for good, but it provides a forum for abuse. Some have interpreted their leadership in an authoritarian fashion. The pastor is no ayatollah. He is not on an ego trip. The pastor's authority is not coercive but given by the Lord. Nevertheless, there is a position of leadership and a function of oversight which must be carried out by God's appointed leader.

For this reason the phrase "have charge over you" is qualified with "in the Lord" (1 Thess. 5:12). Administrative leadership is a spiritual authority exercised in the Lord. The pastor's leadership is the old-fashioned kind in that it is "earned." The pastor's authority is given by God and earned through service. The pastor is both leader and servant. This presents a unique dilemma, requiring the pastor to be powerful and humble at the same time. Yet surely this is the leadership model provided by the Lord Jesus. He stooped to wash the disciples feet, yet He was clearly the leader of the disciples. His leadership of the twelve was never in question.[4] Many pastors are willing to be servants, but they are reluctant to be overseers or leaders.

The fact that leadership offers the potential for abuse does not mean that we can ignore the need for strong pastoral leadership. The pastor must fulfill this role, and the church must follow his leadership.

We live in a day when people are reluctant to accept authority and structure. We chafe at the idea of someone having authority over our lives. Add to this natural reluctance to submit to leadership the fear of an authoritarian, dictatorial rule, and we can understand why some churches have rejected all pastoral leadership. But neither the abuse of authority, nor the aversion to authority should cause us to reject God's design for the church. In Hebrews 13:15-17, one of the clearest passages on the sacrifices offered by the community of priests (priesthood of believers), we are instructed: "Obey your leaders, and submit to them; for they keep watch over your souls, as those who will give an account. Let them do this with joy and not with grief, for this would be unprofitable for you." The matter of pastoral leadership has become both theological and sociological. We must not compromise theological truths because of sociological accomodation.

Many pastors have added to this dilemma by neglecting the biblical responsibility for overseeing the life and mission of the church. This has left many churches floundering for direction and literally perishing from the lack of vision. Administration is not an easy task, and most pastors prefer to preach and visit, duties that provide more immediate results and feedback. C. Peter Wagner believes that many pastors fail to accept leadership responsibilities because they were not trained to do so in seminary. He observes that during the sixties and seventies, seminaries taught pastors to be enablers and not leaders. They taught the pastor that he was a member of the body, not a leader of the body. He further argued that this overemphasis on the enabler role of the pastor, to the exclusion of the leadership role, had been a factor in the epochal decline in church membership since 1960.[5] The pastor must accept his biblical responsibility and function as overseer of the church. While the pastor is one gifted member among many, he is gifted and called to lead. We must not minimize the pastor's leadership role.

In other cases, churches have actually usurped this area of the pastor's responsibility. I think, more often than not, this has happened by default because pastors come and go with great rapidity, particularly in small church fields. (Recent statistics from one denomination reveal that the average tenure for a pastor is thirty-one months.) The deacons or some other group feel the need to provide administrative stability. Whether the pastor abdicates or the church grasps the authority, the church generally pays the cost in terms of a lack of clear direction. When a church calls a pastor, they must look for that individual whom they can trust to lead them and then follow, love, and encourage. In turn the pastor must lead "in the Lord."

Exercising pastoral leadership does not mean authoritarian or dictatorial control. The pastor is a servant/leader. Members and leaders exercising different functions share responsibility in the church. Hammering out these proper roles and relationships takes time and trust. Be patient. It is worth the time and the energy required to establish proper relationships and functions so that the church will be most effective in fulfilling its mission. This is not an issue of favored *status*, either with God or men, but a matter of *function* so the church will be fully empowered for service.

The concept of pastoral leadership in no way negates the truths of the priesthood of believers, the gifted body, nor the congregational structure of the church. All the members, including the pastor, are gifted to serve. The pastor is gifted to lead and therefore, called out by God to function in this position of authority. The Bible clearly teaches shared ministry, but this must not be confused with shared authority. We have a wonderful example of pastoral leadership and shared ministry in action in Acts 6. The pastoral needs of a growing church outstripped the ability of the apostles to meet those needs and give sufficient attention to prayer and teaching the Word. The apostles therefore developed a plan for shared leadership involving other Spirit-empowered persons in the church. The apostles presented their plan for shared ministry to the congregation who approved it and elected those who would serve as deacons.

Instruction

If the New Testament gives one area of the pastor's responsibility greater weight, it appears that it would be that of instruction. In the narrative of Acts 6 the apostles refused to neglect the ministry of the Word for the serving of tables. They gave a priority to their teaching ministry. In 1 Timothy 3:2, "able to teach" is a priority qualification for one who desires the office of overseer. In that same letter Paul declared that those who work hard at preaching and teaching are worthy of double honor (5:17).

In Ephesians 4:11-16, the pastor/teacher is given to the church to equip the saints for the work of ministry. Here is a vital connection between gifted members and those called to leadership. The leaders function in a manner to equip and enable the believers to discover, develop, and utilize their spiritual gifts for the good of the body. The end result of such cooperative ministry will be unity (v. 13), maturity (v. 13), doctrinal stability (v. 14), and the growth of the body in love (v. 16). If churches are going to grow and fulfill their mission, we must recapture the biblical vision of the servant/pastor who is gifted to lead the congregation and equip the laity to do their part in accomplishing the goals and mission of the church.

A Question of Titles

Titles hold a certain fascination for people. In the business world, people often take a promotion primarily for the sake of the title. It stands to reason, therefore, that we are inquisitive about titles in the New Testament church. I am frequently asked why our church does not have elders or bishops. That is a fair question and deserves an answer.

I would preface my remarks by saying that the New Testament church was less concerned with titles than we are today. In the New Testament the emphasis was on *function* rather than *status*. Jesus certainly modeled this as an ideal for the church with His consistent emphasis on servanthood as the model for leadership. It was not important to the New Testament community that those who served in various leadership capacities be given titles. Even when they were given titles, it seems likely that these titles may have differed from location to location.

Yet we can identify three primary descriptive terms used in the New Testament to describe the function of those who occupied leadership positions. The word *elder* translates the Greek *presbuteros.* "Pastor" translates *poimēn,* while "overseer" translates *episkopos.* The term *elder* comes from a Jewish background. You will recall that Jesus was asked why His disciples didn't obey the traditions of the elders (Matt. 15:2; see Ex. 17:6). It is likely that "elder" was used as a title more frequently in early Christian communities, which were predominately Jewish.

The word *pastor* describes the function of a shepherd. Included are such ideas as laboring among, nurturing, protecting, and providing for the feeding of the flock. It may well be that the use of this term to describe the work of the leader came from the teaching of Jesus concerning Himself as the Good Shepherd (John 10). Many churches today seem to prefer the term *pastor* as a title for their leader.

The word *episkopos* is better translated "overseer" rather than "bishop." It was not a title, but a description of function. As discussed above, it described the administrative work of the pastor.

These three terms were not titles referring to two or three different individuals, but rather they are descriptions of the several functions of a single individual. Look, for example, at Acts 20. In verse 17, we discover that Paul had called the elders of the church at Ephesus to meet with him at Miletus. In verse 28, we read that Paul gave the elders the following charge: "Be on guard for yourselves and for all the flock, among which the Holy Spirit has made you *overseers*, to *shepherd* the church of God which He purchased with His own blood" (author's italics). Notice that the elders are called to shepherd and to oversee. All three Greek terms mentioned above are used in this one passage to describe one group of individuals.

Another instructive passage is 1 Peter 5:1-2. Peter addressed himself to the elders. He exhorted them to "*shepherd* the flock of God among you, *exercising oversight*" (AT). Here again we find all three terms in a single context. Notice, too, if you would, that pastoral leadership is not a matter of authoritarian dictatorship. The elders do not lead by "lording it over those allotted to your charge," but rather by "proving to be examples to the flock" (v. 3). Once again we are thrust back to a servant model for leadership.

One final instructive passage is 1 Timothy 5:17. Paul spoke of the elders who rule well and work hard at preaching and teaching. Different Greek words are used, but the elder is still described in terms of his function as overseer and teacher.

Qualifications (1 Tim. 3:6-7)

With such great responsibility and visibility, we must ask what qualifications are required of one who would aspire to do the work of the overseer. Obviously, in such short space we can take only a cursory look at the qualifications. They certainly deserve a much more detailed study. Yet we cannot leave this important topic without at least a few comments. It is true in this case that to whom much is given, much is required. The pastor, by virtue of his work, is given a position with high profile in the community. In a sense, to many people, he represents the church. His position gives him access to confidential and highly personal information. His ministry of pastoral care provides him with opportunities for ministry when people are hurting and their defense system is down. Thus there are opportunities for great good and great harm. It is essential therefore that the pastor be an individual above reproach, both in the church and the community at large.

Life-Style and Family Relationships

Instead of looking at each individual word, let's just focus on major areas of concern. You will notice that the overseer's work requires that he be "hospitable," "able to teach," and able "to manage his own household" (v. 5). The management of the household is immediately related to the ability to "take care of the church of God" (v. 5). We have again discovered the threefold focus of shepherding (here through hospitality), teaching, and administrating. Thus, these qualifications relate to the pastor's ability to function effectively in the primary areas of God-given responsibility.

Two other closely related concerns are the pastor's life-style and his family relationships. The overarching concern is that he must be above reproach. This finds expression through words such as temperate, prudent, and respectable; these ideas indicate a balanced life-style that embodies strict moral values. The pastor cannot be a person whose life-style is marked by excess in any area. He cannot be controlled by wine. Like the Nazarites of the Old Testament, he must be in control of his faculties at all times. I think that there can be a strong biblical case made for total abstinence for the purpose of witness and ministry, but this passage does not say as much.

The pastor cannot be quarrelsome or argumentative. He must be free of excessive attachment to money. This is required of both pastor and deacon. Probably the requirement was related to their responsibility for the collection and distribution of funds to the poor and needy. This verse should not be used to keep the pastor as poor and humble as the proverbial "church mouse." We must balance this verse with 1 Timothy 5:17, which recommends "double honor" for those who work hard at preaching and teaching. "Double honor" likely refers to financial remuneration.

The pastor must have positive family relationships with his wife and his children. The phrase "husbands of only one wife" has been taken in several different ways: (1) not polygamous, (2) married only once (separation caused by death), (3) married only once (separation caused by divorce), (4) a married man, (that is, not single), or (5) faithful to his wife. Scholars have not been able to conclusively resolve this interpretative dilemma after many generations of research. Anyone who attempts to be dogmatic about one interpretation is treading on thin ice. We know, for example, that Paul himself ministered while single. It is very possible that Paul was married prior to his conversion and that his Jewish wife left Paul because of his conversion to Christianity. That would make 1 Corinthians 7:7-15 somewhat of a personal testimony. We also know that Paul encouraged widows(ers) to remarry under certain conditions. The first or last suggestions above appear to be the more likely options. Instead of trying to resolve a complex problem, let's look at the positive point that can be affirmed by all readers of this text. Paul was emphasizing that the pastor, if married, should be a happily married individual whose personal family life was in order. This command is certainly relevant in our day. All too often pastors get so busy in the Lord's work that they neglect their own homes. The pastor simply runs out of energy before he gets home. This inevitably leads to the dissipation and destruction of a pastor's effectiveness and his marriage. For the sake of our family and our church, we must embody those principles concerning marriage that we preach to others.

Not only must the pastor be happily married, he must manage his own household in an orderly fashion. This would certainly include such matters as finances and personal goals. I continually find laypersons and churches who have been hurt by a pastor who neglected to pay bills or whose personal finances were in total disarray. This too is a part of our witness. The pastor must keep his children under control with *all dignity*. I've often thought that the Lord exercised a great sense of humor when he added the small phrase, "with all dignity" (1 Tim. 3:4). I often notice lay people watching when the pastor's kids go climbing over the pews. I know what they're thinking! *Let's see him handle this one with dignity!* The pastor's home is his place of haven, love, and support; therefore, it must reflect the dignity, love, and spiritual maturity that the pastor would seek to develop in the church.

I can testify to the very central role of the home in my own ministry. I grew up in a pastor's home where both my mom and dad practiced these principles. I never felt neglected for the church. Warmth, love, and balance were always present in my boyhood home. My wife, Paula, and my children are the greatest stabilizing force of my own ministry. My home is the place where I am at once most comfortable and vulnerable. When I begin to feel self-important, my family helps to give me that much needed perspective. To my children, I'm not an author or conference speaker; I'm just Daddy. Here I sense true release and refreshment. Most of the credit is due to my wife who is without question a model of a helpmate. I know with absolute assurance that, were it not for the safety and stability of my home, I could not face the day-to-day rigors of my work.

Pastors know about the centrality of the home, and we preach convincing sermons about family life; but in truth many of us are not very sensitive to our own families. We fail to practice what we preach. I know from personal experience. I was fresh on the field in Norfolk, and the church had begun to explode with growth. We had very little staff, and I was in constant demand. Everyone sympathized with me for the hours I had to keep. I dutifully nodded in agreement, but inside I was eating it up. I wanted to be needed and the more often, the better. It fed my ego.

During that first year, our third daughter was born. There was no let up at the church and thus little time for the family. One day I received a phone call from my wife. She started the conversation with a simple statement. "Ken, I know of a family in our church that's in trouble. They need you to see them now. It's an emergency!"

I looked at my full calendar for the day, and I mentally started to juggle it to meet this pressing need. I could make time for this emergency. "Who is it," I responded, "I can go right away."

"Yours," a broken voice uttered.

It's true; I almost shattered my own family while busily looking after everyone else's family. What's worse, I hadn't even seen the signs. The pastor must manage his household well.

Spiritual Maturity

The pastor must, of course, demonstrate spiritual maturity and, therefore, he should not be a new Christian. With authority, there is the danger of pride. This sense of pride could lead to sin, even as it did in the devil's case, and thus bring reproach upon the pastor and the church. Here again the issue is clear. The task of the church is so vital we must have leaders who are willing to live their public and private lives beyond reproach. While this is certainly true of all Christians, it is especially true for the pastor because of the public nature of his work. Our work is too vital to allow for compromise concerning God's standards for leadership.

"King of the mountain" doesn't do justice to the leadership of the church or the biblical concept of the pastor. The issue for the pastor has little to do with titles or power or status. Pastoral authority is given by God, but is earned through positive biblical leadership evidenced by servanthood. Strong pastoral leadership is essential to healthy church growth. When exercised positively, it will not be a constant struggle to keep other vying parties dethroned. The church is the body of Christ, created by God, and working harmoniously as leaders and members serve together according to their God-given abilities. The Bible is clear about shared ministry. Many folks seem to confuse that with shared authority. In the church, we are not seeking to wield authority but to function properly according to our gifts and the responsibility accompanying them. We must lovingly embrace God's structure for the church.

No "king of the mountain" here!

Notes

1. For a more complete discussion of 1 Thessalonians 5:12-21, see Kenneth S. Hemphill, *Spiritual Gifts: Empowering the New Testament Church* (Nashville: Broadman Press, 1988).

2. George Gallup, "Worldwide Trends in Religion" (Speech given at the Biennial Meeting of the Lausanne Committee for World Evangelization, Atlanta, 22 January 1987), 2.

3. The final two occurrences are in Titus and are much more general, meaning nothing more than "promoting" good works (3:8,14).

4. C. Peter Wagner *Leading Your Church to Grow* (Ventura. Calif.: Regal Books, 1984), 80-83.

5. Ibid., 47-48.

13

Jacks

Now at this time while the disciples were increasing in number, a complaint arose on the part of the Hellenistic Jews against the native Hebrews, because their widows were being overlooked in the daily serving of food. And the twelve summoned the congregation of the disciples and said, "It is not desirable for us to neglect the word of God in order to serve tables. "But select from among you, brethren, seven men of good reputation, full of the Spirit and of wisdom, whom we may put in charge of this task. "But we will devote ourselves to prayer, and to the ministry of the word." And the statement found approval with the whole congregation; and they chose Stephen, a man full of faith and of the Holy Spirit, and Philip, Prochorus, Nicanor, Timon, Parmenas and Nicolas, a proselyte from Antioch. And these they brought before the apostles; and after praying, they laid their hands on them.

—Acts 6:1-6

Did you ever play jacks as a child? I don't see the game around much today with all the sophisticated robots and computerized toys. It seems to have been forgotten. I can't say that it was my favorite game, and I was never very good at it. I could never beat the girls in my neighborhood, so I just quit playing.

Jacks was relatively simple as were most of the games of my childhood. All that was needed were ten jacks (starlike metal objects) and one small rubber ball. The jacks were cast out on the pavement to begin the game. The player would throw the ball into the air, scoop up one jack, and catch the ball in the same hand before the ball bounced twice. During each turn the player attempted to pick up an additional jack, two, three, four, and so forth without dropping those already in hand. At some point my little stubby hand couldn't hold the jacks and catch the ball, and I would be eliminated from the game. I found it frustrating because I needed another hand to hold all those jacks. They just slipped through my fingers.

When we get serious about being the church, we'll soon confront a very real and critical question: 'How does a church grow and yet maintain a personal and caring touch in its ministry?' Where can we find that other hand to keep the additional jacks from slipping through our fingers? Does the New Testament provide a pattern that can be used in the church today? This is obviously a very valid concern. Everything we have studied about the church indicates it is God's desire that the church continue being built. We must reach out to the unsaved and unchurched in our communities. This will inevitably produce growth. Yet we want our ministries to remain personal and caring. We want to ensure that we nurture those whom God entrusts to our care.

There's certainly good news at this point. We do have a New Testament model to address this need. The Christian community in Jerusalem grew rapidly. The inaugural baptismal service of about three thousand persons was an excellent beginning for a new church. Doubtless many of those baptized on the Day of Pentecost were from the surrounding areas (see Acts 2:9-10) and returned to their homeland after the celebration of Pentecost. Nonetheless, as we read the Acts account subsequent to the Pentecost event, we discover that the group of believers in Jerusalem continued to grow: "The Lord was adding to their number day by day those who were being saved" (2:47). "And all the more believers in the Lord, multitudes of men and women, were constantly added to their number" (Acts 5:14).

Yet this growth did not alter the desire of this community to experience a deep level of fellowship and personal caring. Acts 2:42 serves as somewhat of a summary verse: "They were continually devoting themselves to the apostles' teaching and to fellowship, to the breaking of bread and to prayer" (see also Acts 2:44-46; 4:32-35). These early believers were devoted to a balanced ministry including teaching, corporate worship and prayer, and fellowship. Note that passages concerning fellowship and the emphasis on continued growth are intertwined. Great fellowship creates a natural climate for evanglistic outreach and church growth. Also evangelism actually creates greater opportunity for fellowship (see chapter 6).

Just how did this early church cope with its rapid rate of growth? How did they maintain a sense of community and nurture community members while they continued to reach out to the unsaved? How did they continue to pick up more members without dropping those already in hand? How can we accomplish these twin concerns?

Historical Setting

I believe that we can find answers both to the historical and present-day question concerning church growth and fellowship by a study of Acts 6:1-7. I have heard numerous sermons on this passage, particularly when the time rolls around for the church to elect its deacons. Often, it seems to me, the historical context that created the need for a deacon ministry is overlooked.

The first verse alerts us to the exciting and challenging opportunity confronting the Christian community in Jerusalem. "Now at this time while the disciples were increasing in number, a complaint arose on the part of the Hellenistic Jews against the native Hebrews, because their widows were being overlooked in the daily serving of food." The disciples were increasing in number, and the ministry needs of the church grew more demanding. The church was experiencing growth pains!

When I was about fourteen years old, my body decided to do all of its growing in about one year. I had been about average size for my age until this particular year. I went out for football every year, and I'll never forget the coaches' surprise when I came back for my junior year at nearly 200 pounds after having reported for tenth grade football at 140 to 150 pounds. Needless to say, this created some problems for our family's clothing and food budget! But that wasn't the growing pain that bothered me. I can remember waking up at night with my joints aching. I knew a great big football player wasn't supposed to cry, but it hurt. I did what any kid does when it hurts, I looked for Mom. She would rub my knees and elbows with a deep-heating ointment, all the time assuring me that there was good news in the midst of this pain. "You're growing," she would say. "You'll be taller in the morning." I think the encouragement helped more than the ointment. There's a lesson here. Growth does produce pain, but it is healthy pain.

It is pain that I'll gladly bear to reach a lost community for Christ.

The particular growth pain the Jerusalem community faced emerged because the apostles could not meet the pressing needs of feeding the widows and still maintain the quality of their ministry of the Word (v. 2). Prejudice also was involved. Notice that the complaint arose on the part of the Hellenistic Jews against the native Hebrews. "Hellenistic Jews" refers to Jews who spoke the Greek language and who had been affected by the Greek culture itself.[1] The strict Jerusalem Jews remained true to the use of Hebrew or Aramaic language and Jewish culture. From the time of the Babylonian captivity (587 B.C.) onward, many Jews lived outside of Jerusalem. A considerable number of the Jewish people chose not to return to Jerusalem when the opportunity was offered under the reign of the Persian king, Cyrus. Often these Jews of the Diaspora (dispersion) were more open to the influence of the Greek culture and, therefore, were viewed by the native Hebrews as being somewhat liberal in their worldview. A number of the Hellenistic Jews now lived in Jerusalem, and some had responded to the gospel, accepting Jesus as Messiah. Thus, this early church was made up of both native Hebrews and Hellenistic Jews.

The specific growth problem the church in Jerusalem faced emerged from the daily serving of food. It is likely that the daily distribution of food was made from the common funds provided by the generous response of fellow believers (Acts 2:44 *ff.*; 4:34 *ff.*). The Jewish community placed a high premium on the ministry to widows and orphans (Ps. 82:1-4), and this same concern was embraced by the early church (see Jas. 1:27; 1 Tim. 5:9 *ff.*). The full understanding of the gospel compels one to meet the physical as well as the spiritual needs of the individual. Evangelism and social ministry are not competitive. They are complementary aspects of the one gospel. The church today must express the gospel through a loving ministry to the underprivileged and the needy. It must find creative means to express this concern according to the specific needs of the community setting.

I often have attempted to recreate this situation in my imagination. Let's presume that Mrs. Timotheus, a Hellenistic Jew, had been overlooked one day in the serving of food. She had been suspicious for some time that the apostolic staff, made up of native Hebrews, didn't really care for the Hellenists in the congregation. She thought they were interested only in getting new members and could care less about the poorer members of the church as a whole. Thus, out of her concern for the church, she ran next door to her closest friend among the Hellenistic widows and shared how hurt she had been over being neglected in the serving of food. Without seeking any clarification for the oversight, she shared her conclusion that the church had gotten so large that unimportant folks like Hellenistic widows didn't matter with the apostolic staff. Her neighbor agreed and then recalled that while she herself had never been skipped in the serving of the food, she was quite confident she was only getting leftovers. These two decided that they needed to survey the other Hellenistic widows to see if they all were encountering this same lack of attention. After all, such a survey would help them know how to pray more effectively. The snowball grew, tempers flared, and feelings were hurt. Could this tension be resolved?

The apostles responded immediately to resolve this tension, preserve the fellowship, and meet the practical needs of the widows. The apostles, however, could not neglect their God-given tasks to take on this additional ministry responsibility. Remember the threefold job description of shepherding, overseeing, and teaching. It would have been physically impossible for the apostles to be faithful to their own calling and to give hands-on attention to the execution of the charitable allocation of food.

This does not suggest that the serving of tables was considered to be unimportant by the early apostles. The meeting of these practical service needs was vital indeed; otherwise, it would not have been brought to the attention of the church as a whole. It was very simply a matter of calling and function. The apostles (leaders) of the Jerusalem church had a different functional task within the structure of the church, and they could not and should not do everything. A law of diminishing return begins to affect leaders' ministry when they attempt to spread themselves too thin. The apostles, under God's leading, knew that they could not possibly fulfill their own responsibility and undertake this huge task of household nurturing alone.

Good news! God had a plan so that the "jacks" wouldn't slip between their fingers.

Out of their administrative role, the apostles proposed a plan for administering the charitable allocation of food. It was not intended for the leader to take primary responsibility for supervising the financial arrangements of the community. Wise pastors today should follow this prudent example. The leaders proposed the plan and presented it to the congregation for approval and development. The congregation elected the actual persons who were to participate in this ministry. Here we see a harmonious blend of congregational polity and pastoral leadership.

At this point, tradition creates a problem for many of us. We have grown up with the idea that the pastor or staff is called to do all the ministry, and the board of deacons is to administrate the church. We actually have reversed the biblical order. Perhaps this emerged because many laypersons felt it was necessary to have seminary training in order to minister effectively to people's needs. Thus they relinquished God-given ministry roles to the professional clergy. Deacons then often assumed more of the administrative tasks of setting the direction and vision of the church because the pastor didn't have time to do both, or simply didn't want to do it. I also suspect that some deacon boards took on a business role because, in their experience, pastors didn't come to stay very long. Therefore, in order to provide stability to the administrative work of the church, the deacons often have felt the need to control the business of the church. Pastors must be willing to invest both time and energy into a long-term ministry, and churches must give the pastors freedom to be the leaders/equippers of the congregation.

This reversal of roles can have detrimental effects on the life of the church. First, the pastor who feels compelled to do all the ministry will neglect his God-given priority of study, prayer, and teaching. Thus the pulpit ministry will suffer, and his personal spiritual walk will be weakened. I frequently hear pulpit committees complain that there is a scarcity of good "preachers" around today. If the pastor does not have adequate time for preparation and prayer, he will not be an effective pulpiteer.

Now a word to the pastor! You cannot neglect the discipline

of regular Bible study and prayer and fulfill your God-given tasks. Many pastors quit studying when they leave seminary. They fail to continue to read good books and do detailed Bible study from the original languages, and they lose the sense of excitement about their own ministry. This may give us some clue to understanding the alarming and increasing rate of pastors leaving the ministry. Burnout is almost certain for the pastor who does not maintain fresh Bible study and a disciplined prayer life. Likewise, the pastor who feels he must control all the ministries of the church is destined for frustration and ministry overload.

Second, the reversal of roles often creates a situation where the pastor is given no freedom to lead the church in developing a strategy for ministry. A fine line of balance must be maintained between pastoral leadership and congregational polity. The pastor is not to be a dictator who drives his people, but he is to be a servant who leads his people. For us to follow a biblical pattern, it will require work on the part of the pastor and the congregation. The pastor must truly be a servant to his community and earn the right to lead by his consistent walk with the Lord and with his people. The people, in turn, must encourage him to lead, be willing to follow, and support his leadership in the midst of successes and failures.

Third, and perhaps the most disconcerting effect of the pastor (staff) doing all the pastoral ministry, is the loss of opportunity for the laity to serve according to their gifts. All believers are gifted for service, thus, when laypersons deprived of God-given opportunities to function according to their gifts for service, the church suffers. The church must be careful to elect deacons who demonstrate gifts for service and then equip them and organize them to serve. We as pastors must take the responsibility for educating the churches on the biblical patterns for deacon ministry. Certainly it must be disconcerting for deacons to make a home or hospital visit only to hear the complaint, "No one from the church visited me." The deacons and the pastor must become colleagues in ministry, working together to provide for the physical, emotional, and spiritual needs of the congregation. God designed the deacon ministry to provide for the nurturing of the growing congregation.

In denominations where a different ministry structure exists, or in churches where deacons are unprepared or unwilling to accept the ministry role, the pastor must find some method of providing for this nurturing ministry. After all, the New Testament was more concerned about "function" than about "title." Every church needs an organized and trained group of laypersons to provide for the growth level of ministry. Those churches that fail to provide it will ultimately fail to grow.

Terminology

While I have consistently maintained that titles were relatively unimportant in the New Testament era, the terminology used in relationship to deacon ministry is worthy of mention. The word *deacon* is virtually a letter-for-letter transliteration for the Greek noun *diakonos.* The original idea was that of "waiting on tables," but this meaning was extended to mean "serving" in a general sense. In secular Greek usage, the word *diakonos* often was used to convey something of inferior status. This makes the New Testament choice of this word all the more significant. Could it be that this word emerged as the word of choice for those growth ministers because of Jesus' emphasis on greatness through servanthood? For example: "The greatest among you become as the youngest, and the leader as the servant" (Luke 22:26). Thus we have a ministry patterned after the servant spirit of our Lord.

Since the words *service* and *servant* can be used for Christian service in general and for all Christians, it is not easy to determine when these words are used to speak of the office of deacon.[2] For example, Paul referred to himself and other apostles as *diakonos* (1 Cor. 3:5; Eph. 3:7). In these cases the word is translated "servant or "minister" (NASB)." Scholars are less sure as to whether the references to Tychicus (Eph. 6:21) and to Epaphras (Col. 1:7) are to be taken as general descriptive terms or as a specific title. First Timothy 3:8 seems clearly to refer to an order of deacons.

Role of the Deacons

What then is the biblical role of the deacon? Some insist that the primary role was that of ministry, such as visiting shut-ins and caring for church families. Others argue for an administrative role for New Testament deacons because they were overseers of the allocation of food to the widows. I believe that both functions are important to the biblical model. In order to provide for the needs of church families, administrative abilities were certainly necessary. Yet we notice that the qualifications given in Acts 6 place an emphasis on the spiritual qualification of the deacons and thus point to the priority of service. The biblical role almost certainly involved more pastoral ministry than we often see today.

Because of the geographic size of the church field at our church, we have organized our deacons to minister through our Sunday School classes. Each deacon serves as a servant-minister for a particular Bible study group. He is their shepherd and minister. Working with the class leaders, he is commissioned to provide for the well being of his small group. You do not need to adopt our model, but you do need to provide for the ongoing nurturing of all the families in your church. Our system is far from perfect, and we continually work to make it more effective. I can tell you that those classes that have deacons who take seriously their family ministry grow more rapidly and maintain a high percentage of attendance to enrollment.

Qualifications

In Acts we notice that a first concern was that the deacons be persons who possessed a good reputation. The church's reputation is closely bound up with that of its deacons. We must be careful, therefore, to choose deacons who are above reproach in terms of life-style, language, attitude, and behavior, both within the church and the community at large.

Second, the deacon must be full of the Spirit. To be full of the Spirit one must be fully surrendered to Christ. This is an ongoing and daily process through which the Christian is empowered for service. In Ephesians 5:18, Paul encouraged all believers to "be continually being filled with the Spirit" (AT).

Third, the deacon minister should be full of wisdom, which is a gift of God and the direct consequence of prayer. "But if any of you lacks wisdom, let him ask of God, who gives to all men generously and without reproach, and it will be given to him" (Jas. 1:5). Notice that these first three qualifications are all spiritual qualifications.

We may be able to detect a fourth qualification in the phrase "whom we may put in charge of this task" (Acts 6:3). By implication, those men would need the administrative skills that would enable them to assume the responsibility for this ministry.

In 1 Timothy 3:8-13, we find several other qualifications listed, and we will notice that they stress sound character and a firm and mature hold on the true faith. These qualifications again suggest that the primary tasks of the deacons were ministerial and financial. The list of qualifications for deacons follow immediately on those for the "overseer" (v. 2) or pastor. The moral requirements are substantially the same as those for the overseers. A unique addition in the case of the men is there must be an absence of talebearing. In the case of the women, backbiting must be ruled out. Either of these faults could have been destructive to the fellowship of the church, particularly in light of the close contact the deacons had with various individuals in need. Apparently, the concern here was for the protection and confidentiality of those receiving diaconate ministry.

On the other hand, "hospitable" and "able to teach" are not required for the deacon (v. 2). This does not suggest that a deacon should not teach in the life of the church. Indeed, if he is gifted to do so, he may well serve in that capacity. We may wonder whether an individual would have sufficient time to prepare and teach and at the same time meet these ministry needs of the families under his charge. Perhaps we have been guilty of spreading our deacons too thin with multiple responsibilities.

Words like "dignity" and not "double-tongued" point to the seriousness of the diaconate ministry (v. 8). The deacon must be an individual who can be serious when the situation dictates. He must be one who can be trusted to speak the truth in love in every situation.

We already have noted that the deacon must at all times be controlled by the Holy Spirit. Therefore he obviously cannot be controlled by alcohol or by money. The deacon, like the Nazarite of the Old Testament, has committed himself to ministry; therefore, he must be in constant control of all his faculties. The deacon must be a good steward in every sense of that word. He must manage his own money well as an example and testimony to the church. He must not be "fond of sordid gain" (v. 8). His position of administering the benevolent allocation would prove some temptation if he had not mastered this area of life. The deacon should demonstrate mature stewardship by his giving through his church.

The phrase "holding to the mystery of the faith with a clear conscience" (v. 9) once again introduces the qualification of spiritual maturity. The word *mystery* is difficult, but it seems usually to convey a sense of awe and wonder at God's redemptive plan (see Rom. 16:26). Thus the "mystery of the faith" could mean (1) the mystery, which is defined by faith in a objective sense (that is, Christian doctrine), or (2) the mystery of faith that is defined by one's own personal allegiance to Christ. In the first instance, the deacons would be required to have sound theological beliefs and a clear conscience. In the second sense, it would mean that the deacons must have a clear conscience concerning their own personal allegiance to Christ. Both certainly should be true, and perhaps we must interpret the ambiguity of the phrase as intentional. If we have to choose one, the evidence of the Pastoral Letters as a whole suggests that "the faith" would best be understood as a body of doctrine. This interpretation is given support in this context where "mystery" is connected to an early confession of faith. Our deacons must be persons with strong doctrinal convictions.

First Timothy 3:11 has created no small measure of difficulty for commentators. Who are the women being addressed, and what was their role in the early church? Several suggestions have been made: (1) the wives of deacons, (2) a separate ministry of deaconesses, or (3) women who were likewise deacons. The first view has been firmly held by many because of the translation of the *King James Version*, which renders this first phrase "Even so must their wives be grave." Yet the Greek word *gunaikas* may be translated "women," and the Greek has no word for the pronoun "their." If we take "women" as a reference to the wives of deacons, we must ask why Paul gave no qualifications or instructions for the wives of the overseers? The Bible gives no evidence for a separate order of deaconesses. The suggestion that there was a separate order of deaconesses is highly unlikely since there is a separate section in 1 Timothy 5 devoted to the ministry of widows.

The passage simply reads, "Women must likewise be dignified" (3:11). While we must avoid dogmatism at this point, I feel the evidence seems to favor the interpretation that Paul was turning his attention to the women who were also deacons. This view is strengthened by the reference to Phoebe as a deacon (*diakonon*) in Romans 16:1. Chrysostom, commenting on this passage in the fourth century, wrote, "Some have thought that this is said of women generally; but it is not so, for why should he introduce anything about women to interfere with the subject? He is speaking of women who hold the office of deacon."[3]

Finally, Paul turned his attention to the family life of the deacon. The requirements here are comparable to those of the overseer. The relationship between husband and wife must be above reproach. The marriage must provide the stable platform for ministry.

The requirements are high, but so are the rewards and the results. The deacons who serve well will receive due respect from the Christian community appropriate to their service. This position of esteem will lead to "great confidence in the faith that is in Christ Jesus" (v. 13).

An effective deacon ministry will enable the church to continue to grow and yet maintain a depth of caring ministry. God does have a plan that will enable the church to reach its community for Christ without neglecting the needs of the saints and forfeiting our fellowship. We can win at our game of spiritual jacks.

Notes

1. "Hellenists" is derived from a Greek verb meaning "to speak Greek." It means to imitate the Greek or live like a Greek. Technically, it can be used of Greeks as well as non-Greeks who had been influenced by Greek speech and culture. The context in Acts suggests that we understand the Hellenists were Jews of the Diaspora as distinct from Jews of Jerusalem.

2. Scholars have debated whether we can speak of the men in Acts 6 as deacons and thus consider this as the institution of the diaconate. Leon Morris provided an excellent survey of the various arguments put forward. He then concluded that the appointment of the seven men in Acts 6 was a temporary measure to meet a particular crisis. Yet the pattern proved to be useful and thus with modifications became a permanent feature of the Christian community. See Leon Morris, *Ministers of God* (London: InterVarsity Press, 1964), 90.

3. Journal of Ecclesiastical History, XIV, 1. For interpretation of "husbands of only one wife," see the discussion of 1 Timothy 3:2 in chapter 12.

14

The Winning Game Plan

So then those who were scattered because of the persecution that arose in connection with Stephen made their way to Phoenicia and Cyprus and Antioch, speaking the word to no one except to Jews alone. But there were some of them, men of Cyprus and Cyrene, who came to Antioch and began speaking to the Greeks also, preaching the Lord Jesus. And the hand of the Lord was with them, and a large number who believed turned to the Lord. And the news about them reached the ears of the church at Jerusalem, and they sent Barnabas off to Antioch. Then when he had come and witnessed the grace of God, he rejoiced and began to encourage them all with resolute heart to remain true to the Lord; for he was a good man, and full of the Holy Spirit and of faith. And considerable numbers were brought to the Lord. And he left for Tarsus to look for Saul; and when he had found him, he brought him to Antioch. And it came about that for an entire year they met with the church, and taught considerable numbers; and the disciples were first called Christians in Antioch.
—Acts 11:19-26

To be quite honest, few of us as children ever worked our way through to complete many games. Someone would get tired or mad and quit, or everybody decided to add up the assets and declare a winner. What then would a winning game board look like? In chess, the loser's king would be laying on its side. In checkers, all the remaining checkers would be of one color. In Red Rover, all the children are gathered on one team. In Old Maids, the loser is left holding the Old Maid card accompanied by loud guffaws. In most games there's only one winner. There can be many losers or just one as with Old Maids. How about the church? How do we determine losers and winners?

My contention has been that many times we are guilty of "playing church." When it is treated as little more than a social club, when its activities become mere rituals, it can indeed bear a striking resemblance to many of the games we played in our childhood. Yet, clearly, church is no game!

Because church is not a game, it is essential that we develop a successful strategy for church growth. A winning game board in the New Testament church must be one that can be shared by all. It should serve as a model for churches of every generation and in any community. Models galore are being suggested by church growth books. Some argue for the megachurch replete with choir, orchestra, parking garages, and the like. Others suggest that we take as a model a more decentralized style of church with house groups meeting throughout the city. Still others suggest a pattern based primarily on social ministries. Some would urge a model with stiff requirements for membership. Many would urge us to move toward a charismatic model with loose structure and a greater emphasis on praise.

Certainly all of these models demonstrate certain strengths, but all exhibit inherent weaknesses. Not all of them can be duplicated easily in every generation and in any community. Often they depend on the strength of the pastor who envisions the style, and they are not easily repeated in other settings. The megachurch, for one, would be a difficult model to follow in a rural setting. Thus for our model we must go back to a New Testament picture and underline certain basic principles that can be followed and applied in every situation, specifically in your situation.

Clearly, the church of our generation needs a healthy model. Major denominations, with few exceptions, have been experiencing either an actual decline or a serious slowdown in their rate of growth. This has occurred in an era when population continues to grow and an alarming explosion in cultic groups testifies to the spiritual emptiness of a generation. How do we break out of this stagnant cycle? What is the key? To see renewal of growth we must begin at the most basic level, that of the local church. The real key, therefore, is you, the individual church member.

Let's look then for a biblical model of a growing church in the Book of Acts. The Book of Acts begins with a universal commission related to church growth. "You shall receive power when the Holy Spirit has come upon you; and you shall be My witnesses both in Jerusalem, and in all Judea and Samaria, and even to the remotest part of the earth" (1:8). This verse serves as a virtual outline for the Book of Acts. The result of the empowering for witness is seen immediately as 3,000 souls are baptized on the Day of Pentecost. The witness of that early group of believers was so effective that the Sanhedrin commanded them not to teach in the name of Jesus (4:18). The growth of the early church was so explosive that the church soon experienced growth pains; and deacons were elected to undergird a growing ministry (Acts 6:1). Yet the gospel had not broken forth from the confines of Jerusalem.

In Acts 8, we discover that the witness finally burst forth into Judea and Samaria. Yet it was not by design, but from necessity. "On that day a great persecution arose against the church in Jerusalem; and they were all scattered throughout the regions of Judea and Samaria, except the apostles" (v. 1). Still a formidable barrier remained before the commission of Acts 1:8 could become reality. This barrier had racial overtones. Those scattered by the persecution were aggressive in sharing their faith, but many of them were not yet prepared to break down the centuries-old barrier and witness to the Gentiles. "So then those who were scattered because of the persecution that arose in connection with Stephen made their way to Phoenicia and Cyprus and Antioch, speaking the word to no one except to Jews alone" (11:19).

The door for outreach to the Gentiles had been set ajar when Peter preached to Cornelius and the Gentiles received the Spirit (Acts 10). With the door of opportunity open, there was still the need for a local church willing to break the mold—to be a model of a mission-centered community. We might have anticipated it would be the community in Jerusalem, but Antioch became the church of choice. We must learn all we can from this church. Here in Antioch was a church that made a difference.

Church with a Passion for Souls (11:19-22)

First we should notice that the church in Antioch placed a high priority on winning people to faith in Jesus Christ. Several clues in the text indicate that this church was inclined toward aggressive evangelistic outreach. Notice that this church was founded by laypersons who had been scattered by the persecution in Jerusalem. Here were families uprooted from their homeland, driven forcibly from the security of home and family. Yet their first priority was to enthusiastically share their faith in Jesus Christ. This compulsion to witness appears to be a characteristic of the early Christians. Stephen, at his stoning, bore witness to his faith. Sometimes it appeared that Paul welcomed imprisonment because of the unique opportunity it afforded him to witness to other inmates or even his captors. Circumstances did not alter the desire of the early Christians to share their faith.

Often we are so obsessed with our securities that we ignore opportunities for witness. In our churches, our security can be our familiar programs. We become so intent on running the programs that we forget their purpose is to bear witness to the Lord Jesus Christ. We forget that our first calling, our passion, must be to see lost persons come to know Jesus Christ as their personal Savior.

The great apostle Paul gave his testimony that he was called to be an ambassador for Christ (2 Cor. 5:20). This entailed a compulsion so intense that it required him to beg people to be reconciled to God. In that passage Paul declared that God had not only reconciled us to Christ, but He has given to us the ministry of reconciliation. The calling to be an ambassador is not just for apostles or pastors. It is for every individual who has been reconciled to God in Christ. Evangelistic outreach is not simply a part of our ministry, it *is* our ministry and our calling. It must penetrate all that we do. The compulsion to see men and women reconciled to Christ is a distinctive of growing churches.

As I was writing this chapter, our nation was following with rapt interest the plight of three whales who were trapped in an ice flow in Alaska. We viewed the heroic and untiring efforts to save these whales from their frigid entrapment. Under the most adverse circumstances, risking their very lives, Eskimos worked night and day to free the whales. This crisis made allies of those who often appear in adversarial roles. We all cheered as Soviet icebreakers steamed to join the effort. All for three whales! Last summer I witnessed a similar phenomenon as dead and dying dolphins began to wash ashore on our Virginia coastline. Volunteers committed hundreds of hours, raised thousands of dollars, and an entire community was stirred and unified by the plight of the dolphins. What would be the impact of the modern-day church if we were equally moved by the plight of men and women trapped in the icy tomb of sin—facing certain and eternal death?

We can see that the church in Antioch had a compassion for souls by their lack of prejudice. Antioch was founded in 300 B.C. and became the capital city of the Seleucid monarchy. When Syria was incorporated into the Roman Empire in 64 B.C., Antioch was the third largest city of the Roman Empire and had a large Jewish population. The Jewish presence in this community made a Gentile ministry a difficult task. The idea of a community where Jew and Gentile would worship together was unheard of. Yet we're told: "Some of them, men of Cyprus and Cyrene, . . . came to Antioch and began speaking to the Greeks also, preaching the Lord Jesus" (11:20).

A true concern for lost persons is so overwhelming that it overcomes artificial barriers like cultural, racial, or class barriers. I taught at Wingate College for a year after returning from England. I had the privilege of teaching an evening class in which many adults from the community attended. We not only talked about Scripture, but we talked about church ministry. One young man was involved in his church's bus ministry. He frequently expressed his excitement at the opportunities this provided to win persons to Christ. One evening he told me that he was considering dropping out of the bus ministry. I couldn't understand this sudden change of heart. As I queried him, he shared that the drivers had been instructed to ignore houses occupied by black families. To him this was unchristian. The gospel was for all. A true compassion for souls must conquer all prejudice.

The text tells us that God Himself gave confirmation to the work of these witnesses: "The hand of the Lord was with them, and a large number who believed turned to the Lord" (11:21). Notice too, if you would, that the phrase "considerable numbers" is repeated in verses 24 and 26. If we're ever going to restore a boldness to our witness, we must put to death this growing revulsion to "numbers." We act as if numbers are bad, that churches who keep statistics are carnal or egocentric. While it is true that David was punished for arrogantly numbering Israel, it is equally true that God commanded Moses to number the people of Israel. We even have an Old Testament book about numbers. I would assume that our Lord intended us to understand that a harvest of a hundredfold is better than a harvest that is only twentyfold. Numbers count when we're talking about souls for the kingdom of God. If I am given the choice to baptize 200 persons yearly or 20 persons, I'll always opt for the 200. Our compassion for lost persons must lead us to be concerned about the quantity and quality of our witness and ministry.[1]

One year during the preseason workouts for a new basketball season in the N.B.A., the newspapers reported that Michael Jordan had walked off the court after having quarreled with his coach. It seems, at least in Michael's version of the story, that his coach had lost count of the score in a practice game. Scrimmage games don't really count! No one records the outcome nor the points scored by the players. Apparently the coach was thinking this way. Michael Jordan had a slightly different view: "If you aren't going to keep the score, why play?" If an athlete is this serious about points that don't really count, we had better get serious about statistics that *do* count. Most of us are interested in numbers that make a difference in our life. We grab the paper to check the scores of our favorite teams. We might look at the stock market figures to see if our holdings are increasing. We certainly pay attention to the numbers in our checkbooks. It's high time we became serious about statistics that really matter, persons being born into the kingdom of God.

A third clue that indicates this church had a passion for souls is found in Acts 13. When God gave them a vision for spreading the gospel through a mission trip, they agreed with God to send Paul and Barnabas. They sent their best! Do we give our best energies to outreach? Our church recently moved part of our evangelistic outreach visitation to Sunday night. Some of our people sacrifice in giving up Sunday night worship, but we have discovered that many unsaved persons are home on Sunday night. This new idea was endorsed heartily by our folks because outreach demands our best.

Church with Strong Leadership (11:11-26; 13:1)

As a whole, the New Testament tells us little about the leaders of various communities. For that reason, we cannot help but be impressed by both the number and diversity of the leaders in Antioch. Barnabas was sent to Antioch by the apostles in Jerusalem and was so moved by what he saw he stayed to give assistance. Barnabas had a unique style of leadership that brought out the best in others. He was a true encourager. It was Barnabas who brought Paul, the former persecutor, to Antioch. He was thus in great measure the one responsible for getting Paul established in the ministry.

I have often wondered how many of us pastors would be as unselfish as Barnabas if we were to confront an Antiochlike situation today? Barnabas had finally discovered a church in the beginning stages of explosive growth. This is the kind of church most pastors can only dream about: a church poised for growth. It's a custom-made reputation maker. If you had been in Barnabas's place, would you have gone to find Paul to pastor this growing church?

Another unlikely leader is Simeon, whose Latin nickname, "Niger," suggests he was a black man from Africa. Some scholars identify Simeon with Simon of Cyrene who assisted Jesus with the cross. Lucius was a common name, and we have no way of further identifying Lucius. Manaen is the Greek form of the Hebrew word for "comforter." This was a title given to boys the same age as royal princes who were brought up with them at court. Luke told us that Manaen had been a companion of Herod the Tetrarch (Acts 13:1).

Thus we have a solid Jerusalem leader, a persecutor turned missionary, a black, a relative unknown, and a man raised with royalty. This church was blessed with a strong and diverse group of leaders. These leaders had the unique ability to cross cultural and racial barriers as great as any we face today. Positive, biblical, pastoral leadership is a key to church growth. Leaders who are willing to challenge the church to courageously follow God's direction are a must. This is old-fashioned leadership: it is "earned," not granted by title or position. Any church that's going to grow must have a pastor willing to labor among, oversee, and equip the saints. Likewise, it must have people who appreciate and esteem highly those whom God has chosen to lead. It must have strong service-oriented deacons and lay people who are willing to take on leadership responsibilities according to their gifts.

Church with a Generous Spirit (11:27-30)

We've been looking at a church experiencing explosive growth. In Acts 11:27-28 we are told that a prophet from

Jerusalem came to Antioch and told the believers of a famine that would occur in the land. The response from the church at Antioch was cheerful, spontaneous, and generous: "In the proportion that any of the disciples had means, each of them determined to send a contribution for the relief of the brethren living in Judea" (11:29). If this famine was to be universal, the Christians at Antioch would be affected by it as well. Yet there was a spontaneous outpouring that came from the heart.

One of the signs of spiritual maturity for the church and for the individual is generosity. Those who have truly encountered God, who spared not His own Son, begin to exhibit a life-style of giving that is characteristic of their Father. Our growth at First Baptist, Norfolk, has been so rapid that often it has been very painful, at least financially. We've literally been in a building program for six of the past eight years. Yet in each of those years, our church has voted to increase the level of our giving to mission causes outside our church. This sort of spirit pervades the growing Christian and the growing church. Our church could not have experienced the great level of growth that it has if it had not been for many generous people who have given spontaneously and sacrificially.

Church with Spiritual Sensitivity (13:2-3)

The vision for a missionary journey was communicated "while they were ministering to the Lord and fasting" (13:2). The word translated "ministering" is from the Greek word *leitourgeō*, from which we get liturgy. The plan for world evangelization was communicated by the Holy Spirit as this great church worshiped the Lord. It may be that this message was given through a prophet or other leader as they shared in worship.

The church has the opportunity and responsibility to minister to the Lord. Exciting worship is a must for the growing church. There are a variety of worship styles. Often a congregation's style of worship depends on tradition and personal preference. Whatever the style, there is no acceptable reason for the worship service being boring. The hour of worship at your local church should be the highlight of the week. How could the praise and adoration of the God of the universe be dull or boring? We must give worship the best of our energies and resources. We cannot neglect our regular opportunities for worship if we are going to experience exciting church growth.

We must ensure that our worship is such that it would allow opportunity for the Holy Spirit to communicate concerning His plans for the church. I have heard folks remark: "We need to pray that the Spirit will anoint our plans." We need to seek those plans that are God's, for they already have the Spirit's anointing. The present text makes it clear (v. 4) that the plan for world evangelization originated with God, not the apostles. The local church was *attentive* and *responsive* to the leading of the Holy Spirit.

One could not imagine at this point that the early Christians stopped to vote on whether or not they should attempt a missionary journey. Nor did they vote on sending Paul and Barnabas. These issues were determined by the Spirit and communicated in prayer. While I would in no wise suggest that the local church should do away with voting or business meetings, I do think we should spend more time praying than voting. Our desire is not to outvote one another but to *discover the will of God* and *be of one mind on the matter*. This happens on our knees in prayer, not on the floor in debate. We have very little textual evidence to suggest that the early church actually voted on anything. We do know that they prayed to discover the Lord's plan for the church. The local church is still the heart of any mission endeavor. Our missionaries come from local churches. They work to establish growing local churches. The prayer and financial support for their work come through local churches. The growing local church must be mission minded.

We confront another significant word that must not be overlooked: "fasting" (v. 2). This practice of withdrawing from the influence of the world in order to make oneself receptive to the commands of heaven has both an Old Testament and New Testament heritage. Fasting demonstrates the serious depth of the prayer life of the church at Antioch. The restoration of prayer to its rightful place of centrality in our church's life is a must. We have heard or preached sufficient sermons to know that prayer is the very breath of the spiritual life. It is direct access to the throne room of heaven. It is the key to spiritual awakening. Yet, we treat it as a stepchild, with little regard to its rightful place. Every church that desires to be pleasing to God must have an effective prayer ministry.

Church with a Great Vision (13:4)

A layman recently joined our church in response to a sermon he heard by a denominational leader. In that sermon, the seminary president indicated there are only three kinds of churches: the undertakers, the caretakers, and the risk takers. The undertaker church has lost its vision for outreach and growth and is experiencing decline as its members become older. The caretaker church has focused inward. The claim is to focus on inreach, but they, too, have lost a vision for reaching the community. Clearly, the caretaking church is destined to become an undertaker. It's only a matter of time. Finally, there are those few churches that are the risk takers; they have a bold vision for reaching their community. I've thought about those three classifications of churches. I have been privileged to pastor a church that was willing to obey God and take a risk to grow. Yet, I have decided that there is no real risk in obedience. If God calls the church to do something, He is able to provide the strength to accomplish it. The real risk is disobedience. Then we risk failing to be the church that Christ rose to empower us to be.

The church at Antioch could certainly be categorized as a "risk taker." The exciting thing here is the size of the vision of the church at Antioch. This was the beginning of world missions. There were little available means of transportation or communication. From a human standpoint, the task of world evangelization might appear to be too large for any church. Antioch could have balked. A missionary journey had never been attempted before! The task was too large! Let Jerusalem do it! We can't afford it! Not our best leaders!

If we're going to produce bold churches, we must eliminate phrases like, "we can't," "never been done that way," and "too expensive." When the Holy Spirit gives a vision, we have only to follow that vision.

I first discovered the power of a vision while I was a student at Southern Seminary. I was pastoring a small rural church in Wolf Creek, Kentucky. One of my seminary professors told us we ought to have a "dream" night. That sounded good to me. I barely had enough material to preach on Sunday morning, so an idea for Sunday night was treasured. The plan was simple. I would announce the "dream night," preach an appropriate sermon, and moderate the evening dream session. The date was set, the sermon preached, and to my absolute surprise the place was packed that evening. After a few songs and a short devotional, I shared the rules. One, you don't have to be able to pay for a dream. Two, you can't contradict someone else's dream. I opened the floor for dreams.

Silence! "Boy," I thought, "this is a stupid idea; nobody's going to talk." After what seemed like hours, someone finally ventured a dream, "Pastor, I think we need to build a basketball court for the kids." Not what I anticipated, but it was a dream. As I quickly reflected on it, I saw it was an outstanding idea. Remember, Kentucky is basketball country. "Great idea!" I responded.

"It is?" he asked, sounding surprised.

This opened the door. "We need a porch on this church." "We need to lay the cornerstone." "A first priority must be indoor bathrooms." You read it right; we were still using those outhouses that were good enough for Granny. Then we dreamed up a youth choir and a bus to go with them. We got around to waterproofing the basement. I could vote for that since I had to help with the mopping every time it rained. We dreamed for over an hour and filled a legal pad with our dreams. Our dream session was a great success.

I was feeling justifiably proud that evening as we headed back down Dixie Highway to our Seminary Village apartment. My self-satisfaction was rudely interrupted by my wife. "What are you gonna do now?"

"Whata-ya-mean?" I spat back.

"You get these people all excited dreaming, now what are you going to do? We don't have the money to do any of those things."

Boy, was I angry. I was angry because she was right. I didn't know what to do. My professor had not gotten to that point yet.

During that week I decided that the quickest and cheapest project was the waterproofing of the basement. I talked to some local contractors and found out how this could be accomplished and what materials would be needed. I announced that this would be our first project. I didn't know you had to vote on little things like this!

A couple of the men agreed to pick up the waterproofing material and the pipe and to have gravel delivered to the church. We would all meet bright and early on the coming Saturday and do the work.

Saturday arrived, and so did the materials, but I was the work party of one. I started to work with a pick and shovel, but I soon decided that I would graduate from seminary before I finished the project. It was then that I had a minor stroke of genius. I had recently baptized a young man who had a terrible reputation in the community. He was so excited about being a Christian, I knew he would do anything. Besides, I had it on pretty good authority that this guy had some experience at breaking rocks. He was delighted to be asked to help. When he discovered it was just the two of us, he volunteered to bring his friends. At this point he only had one kind of friends. Talk about a chain gang, I had one!

We started to work right in the very front of the church. It wasn't long before word spread about this "select" work crew. I began to notice an increase in the volume of traffic in front of the church. Pickup truck after pickup truck rolled slowly past. Soon our work party began to grow, and by lunch a deacon with a backhoe arrived. We completed our first dream that Saturday, but that's not the whole story.

One of the men said, "Why don't we do the basketball court next?" This guy wasn't even a member. News travels fast in small communities. He had a vested interest: his sons. "I can finish concrete," he stated. It was decided: this was to be our next project. This did create a small dilemma. The supplies for a basketball court involved substantial money; we only received about $100 a week, and I received $50 of that. It sure was good I didn't know we had to vote on projects like this, or pray for dreams. By the time we were ready to build the court, we had been given sufficient money. We completed our second dream.

In eighteen months we had completed every item on our dream list. There were greater benefits. During that eighteen-month period, fifty-three persons accepted Christ and were baptized. What happened? We dared to dream a great dream!

Look again at our Antioch model. The church responded to the dream immediately. It's God's work! Too big for human beings? Sure! But comfortably within the realm of "All things are possible"! We're too willing to accept second best and to ask God for too little.

My wife enjoys reading and frequently draws my attention to interesting articles. On one occasion we both became interested in a series of stories about whales. These whales were actually swimming up onto the beach and dying. No one could determine the cause of this peculiar behavior. Some theorized that the whales were exhibiting a behavior similar to that of elephants who wander off to secret burial grounds to die. Yet this sort of behavior had never been seen in whales before. As the inquiry of the scientific community progressed, whales continued to die on the beach. Finally, the riddle of their destructive behavior was solved. They discovered that the huge mammals of the sea were themselves to blame. Food had apparently been scarce in the normal feeding areas. The whales began to chase sardine-sized fish, and in so doing the whales had unwittingly followed them into a shallow cove. They became so busy feeding on the small fish that they failed to notice that the tide was going out. As the tide receded, the whales were marooned in the shallow water. Ultimately, they washed ashore and died.

We are seeing the skeletons of churches that have occupied themselves with sardine-sized issues. They've focused and fussed about little issues and have failed to pay the price to dream a great dream. They now lie beached and bloated. We cannot waste the great power of God's church on small dreams. No dream is too great for the church. We must boldly move out on mission to reach the world for Jesus Christ. God has given us in Christ Jesus a winning game board. Let's learn from this great model church in Antioch. These principles will work in your church.

Notes

1. For a more detailed discussion of the purpose of numbers, see Ken Hemphill and R. Wayne Jones, *Growing an Evangelistic Sunday School* (Nashville: Broadman Press, 1989).

15

Putting Away the Game Board

"Go therefore and make disciples of all the nations, baptizing them in the name of the Father and the Son and the Holy Spirit, teaching them to observe all that I commanded you; and lo, I am with you always, even to the end of the age."

—Matthew 28:19-20

Y ou kids put the game board away! The game is over now!"
Those words have a familiar ring. With every game there
comes a time when we have to fold up the game board, put
away the playing pieces, and get back to the real world.

Although we often go about our activities and responsibilities at church as if they were little more than religious play,
church is no game. If there is any place where we should deal
with issues that matter in people's lives, it should be in the
church. We must address real-life issues, such as human sexual-
ity, marriage, divorce, pain, separation, depression, and death.
We must grasp the staggering truth that what we do in the
body of Christ not only matters now, but it determines where
people will spend eternity. For these reasons, we must put up
our church game board. Too much is at stake to pretend that
we have fellowship or to play at worship or to talk about strate-
gies for outreach. We hold the keys to the Kingdom! We must

quit playing games and give the very best of our time, energy, and financial resources to the one community that has eternity at stake.

Take Up the Cause

We began this study with a look at Jesus' bold declaration, recorded in Matthew 16:13-20, that He was going to build a messianic community, eternal in nature, to whom He would entrust the keys of the Kingdom. In the context of that announcement Jesus also revealed "that He must go to Jerusalem, and suffer many things from the elders and chief priests and scribes, and be killed, and be raised up on the third day" (Matt. 16:21). The disciples were not yet able to understand that such an apparent disaster could be part of God's plan. Peter, the very one who confessed, "Thou art the Christ, the Son of the living God," was the one to object. Jesus thus rebuked Peter for not setting his mind on God's interests. He was thinking with only human consideration. Jesus addressed all His disciples when He clarified the demands of discipleship. To follow Jesus, to be a part of His forever family, means that we must be involved in His redemptive work. We must literally deny ourselves and take up His cross. The taking up of the cross demands a total commitment to His redemptive work. To deny ourselves is not a call for mild asceticism or minimal sacrifice: it means disciples must renounce all rights to their own lives. We are His, bought with a price and empowered to serve Him. Consequently, we forfeit all claims to our own time, money, and gifts, for they are already His—purchased by His death on the cross. These verses remind us that this is no game, and that we are faced with a fundamental choice concerning both our allegiance and the investment of our total resources either for Him or for ourselves.

As we approach this final passage in Matthew's Gospel, we are aware that the crucifixion and resurrection have become reality. The seeming defeat of Golgotha has been transformed into the triumph of Galilee. This resurrection appearance becomes the basis for the commission of the church that will last "to the end of the age."

Commissioned with Authority

The eleven disciples, minus Judas, proceeded to the mountain in Galilee that had been specified by Jesus before His death (26:32; see 28:10). The mountain was not specifically named, but it was intended to call to mind Jesus' teaching ministry in Galilee. Thus the wider mission of Jesus through His church was to be launched where the original mission began. Matthew desired for us to understand that the work of the eleven was clearly continuous with that of Jesus Himself. The eleven were apparently alone, but here, as they often did, they represented the whole company of Jesus' brethren. Our work too is continuous with that of the mission of Jesus.

They first saw Jesus at a distance, and their joy and praise collided with the uncertainty and fear. Their first reaction was to worship, but the whole of the event was so overwhelming that "some were doubtful" (28:17). Some of the disciples, like Thomas, took longer to accept the reality of the resurrection. To reassure them, Jesus came and spoke to them.

Jesus first assured them with a magnificent declaration concerning His universal authority. This passage takes on even deeper meaning when we recognize that the claim is based on the promise of Daniel 7:14. Jesus quoted this passage as recorded in Matthew 26:64 in response to the high priest's query as to whether He was the Messiah, the Son of God. Jesus responded: "You have said it yourself; nevertheless I tell you, hereafter you shall see the Son of Man sitting at the right hand of power, and coming on the clouds of heaven." That which only a few days ago was "hereafter" had now come to pass. Thus the prophecy that the Son of Man would be exalted as sovereign ruler was fulfilled in the resurrection. Jesus exhibited authority during His earthly ministry, but now He has received *all* authority. It is *all* authority that forms the basis for a mission to *all* nations, a commission to teach *all* things, and assurance that He will be with them *always*. Paul repeated this same theme in Ephesians 1:22-23 where he declared: "He put all things in subjection under His feet, and gave Him as head over all things to the church, which is His body, the fulness of Him who fills all in all." With such authority, how can we ever consider playing church?

The universal dominion of Christ demands a universal mission for the church, His body. We must first accept the fact that His commission is binding. It is not a suggestion given to the church. It is no option. Christ's commission is the marching order of the church until the end of the age. The overarching command is to make disciples of all nations. "Going," "baptizing," and "teaching" translate Greek participles that are dependent on the main verb "make disciples." Thus going, baptizing, and teaching are integral to the discipling process. The phrase "of all the nations" reminds us of a constant theme of this gospel that God desires to call out a people in which membership is based on a relationship with God through His Son rather than on race or nationality.

All too often we have seen this verse only in the context of world missions; therefore, we have failed to see its relevance to the task of the local church. We feel that we have obeyed this commission if our church gives money to world mission causes. We certainly ought to give, and we ought to go. We must develop a mind-set and conviction for reaching the world. The church that fails to look with responsibility beyond its own local community will become introverted and die. A mission emphasis is essential to the ongoing life of a growing church.

Nevertheless, it is my conviction that the Great Commission must also be fulfilled in the work of the local church as it makes disciples in its own sphere of responsibility. I believe that the most effective tool for accomplishing the threefold task of the Great Commission is the Sunday School, the age-graded small-group Bible study of the church. Simply stated, the goal is to fulfill the Great Commission through the local church. All too often we have understood our small-group Bible study program only in terms of a teaching ministry.

Make Disciples

What does it mean to make disciples? How does one go about it? Where do we start? All good questions. Often when I hear people talk about making disciples they mean "maturing believers" or "polishing spiritual apples" that have already been harvested. I occasionally hear an unmistakable echo of this sort of thinking when pastors or laypersons insist that their church is interested in discipleship and not evangelism.

We must destroy this unbiblical distinction. The raw material for making disciples is unbelievers. That is certainly the implication of the command to "go" and make disciples. Any concordance will reveal that the word *disciple* occurs in the New Testament only in the Gospels and the Book of Acts. If discipling meant the maturing of believers, we would expect this term to occur frequently in the Pauline Letters where Paul addressed himself to the ongoing life of the church community.

Go

We must quit playing the church game and accept that the Great Commission requires that we go out into our community and into the world at large to win those who are lost. We must use every means at our disposal to make disciples. Evangelism training is a must for all local churches in every community. People are unlikely to share their faith if they are not given specific training and actual practice. Sufficient training materials are on the market today to eliminate all excuses. We must use every creative effort at our disposal to reach out into the community. For too long, we in the church have been guilty of waiting for the lost world to come to us. We must penetrate our community if we are going to fulfill the Great Commission in our church setting.

Our church has discovered that music is an excellent tool for penetrating the secular community. Here again it may require that we take the music out of the church and into the community. For years we have held our Christmas musical at a civic auditorium. We found the unsaved more open to attending. Shopping malls are open to quality music groups, particularly during the holiday season. Many good books that tell of innovative evangelistic ideas are available. The component most lacking is not method but *commitment* to do the task. The church must accept *making disciples* as our God-given priority.

We may very well be overlooking our best outreach tool when we neglect the role of the Sunday School for reaching the lost. Generally Sunday School is the organization with the greatest structure in the church. It is the natural place for outreach to occur. Christians who are not yet trained to share their faith can use the Sunday School by enrolling their unsaved friends in their class. A common statistic used in church growth conferences is that two out of three unsaved persons who regularly attend small-group Bible study will make a commitment to Christ in the first twelve to eighteen months.

Many Sunday School leaders do not see evangelism as a part of the task of the Sunday School. Their attitude can best be summarized: "Pastor, you reach them, and we'll teach them." Yet those who have been instrumental in making the Sunday School a central element of life clearly understand the evangelistic role of the Sunday School. Gaines Dobbins wrote: "The Sunday School is the arm of the church best suited to reach out into the community and both find and fetch the unreached and unchurched. It is a truism that 75 to 80 percent of the additions of the average evangelical church come through its Sunday School."[1] One must wonder if Dr. Dobbins's statistics remain valid today?

Even a cursory look at the Book of Acts reveals the valuable role of teaching and evangelism. In Acts 4:2 we find that the Jews were greatly disturbed because "they were teaching the people and proclaiming in Jesus the resurrection from the dead." The Sanhedrin censured the disciples and demanded that they not teach in the name of Jesus (Acts 4:18). The famous story of the conversion of the Ethiopian eunuch reveals the key role of teaching the Scriptures in evangelistic outreach. If we truly believe that the Word of God is the power of God unto salvation, then we must not continue to overlook the role of the Sunday School in the ongoing outreach of the church.

When I was nine years old, our family moved to Thomasville, North Carolina, to accept a new pastorate. We left a beautiful, brick church building in the mountains for a rather tattered facility overlooking a lumberyard. In a few years, my dad had led that church to relocate on a lovely new sight. One afternoon my dad and I stopped by to walk over the construction site. The foundation had been laid, and the block work had just begun. It didn't look like much to me, but my father could visualize the completed building. We walked through the sanctuary, pausing for a moment to stand behind the pulpit. My dad then turned and looked toward the educational plant. He paused for a moment, and the running commentary of the guided tour ceased. Thinking about the Sunday School rooms, he reflected: "I can remember the time that nearly everyone who was won to Christ came through our Sunday School, but no more. It seems like I'm the only one doing outreach, and thus people have a loyalty to me and the worship service but not the Sunday School." I didn't fully understand the implications of his statement that day, but I am beginning to understand it more clearly.

I would challenge readers of every denominational background to check your own statistics related to small-group Bible study and the effectiveness of your outreach. Probably you will find that growth in Sunday School enrollment is an accurate barometer for your effectiveness in outreach. Sunday School growth has been nearly flat since 1960, and baptisms continue to decline yearly. We must shake our lethargy and restore evangelism to its rightful place in our churches and particularly in our Sunday Schools.[2] We must "go" if we are going to be effective at making disciples.

Baptize

Baptism was, and is, a key element of making disciples. Baptizing in the Gospels is most often associated with the ministry of John the Baptist, yet it was, apparently, a characteristic part of Jesus' own ministry through His disciples (John 3:22-26; 4:1-3). John's baptism was preparatory (John 1:25-34), for a fuller, more meaningful baptism that would be inaugurated by the coming Messiah. The Messiah's baptism of the believer in the Holy Spirit occurred at the new birth and expressed the disciple's commitment to the Father through the Son. Jesus commissioned His disciples to baptize in the name of the Father, the Son, and the Holy Spirit.

The first Christian baptismal service occurred on the Day of Pentecost. "So then, those who had received his word were baptized; and there were added that day about three thousand souls" (Acts 2:41). The context fleshes out the implications of baptism. Not only does baptism represent incorporation into Christ but, of necessity, the incorporation into His body, the church. Therefore, it is not surprising that the next verse explains they were "continually devoting themselves to the apostles' teaching and to fellowship, to the breaking of bread and to prayer."

I think it is fair to say that we could legitimately discuss baptism in terms of becoming a part of the body of Christ. It not only signifies the believer's new birth, but it further indicates that by virtue of this birth one has been incorporated into a community of believers—"his forever family." We have not fulfilled the requirements of our commission to make disciples by baptizing them when we merely get persons into the baptistry. We fulfill the demand to baptize when we lead the new convert to express commitment to Christ in a visible and public way and to become part of a body of committed believers. We must lead new believers to express their faith in Christ by an active identification with His church.

Christian conversion marks a critical juncture. There is the breaking of old habits and the discarding of old values for new. Often it means leaving old friends. The new believer needs the personal support of his or her new family.

Here again the small-group context of the Sunday School provides the most effective unit for follow-up, fellowship, and the assimilation of new converts. No other single factor is more important for conserving the results of evangelism than an effective Sunday School that has been prepared to do follow-up.

Our church is presently moving to a Sunday School organizational system whereby a deacon serves as a family minister to a specific Sunday School class. The deacon coordinates the work of the care leaders to ensure that everyone is regularly contacted and that spiritual needs are being met by the church. The Sunday School provides the most natural setting for this caring ministry. The Sunday School class is a manageable size. Friendships are established as members meet together for Bible study every Sunday morning. This setting enhances and encourages the fellowship and nurturing of all members of the class. This plan also enables the pastor and/or staff to be aware of ministry needs more quickly. Once again we find the Sunday School to be the place for incorporating folks into the life of the church.

Teach Them to Obey All Things

Up to this point in Matthew's Gospel, Jesus alone was the Teacher. The verb "to teach" previously had not been used by Matthew to describe the work of the disciples.[3] The disciples were to extend the teaching ministry of Jesus. They did not simply espouse abstract ideas, but they taught those they led to Christ "to observe all that I commanded you" (v. 20). We can never say that making disciples has been completed until we lead believers to a life of obedience to all Jesus' commandments. The ultimate goal of the church must be that we render every person mature in Christ, "that the man of God may be adequate, equipped for every good work" (2 Tim. 3:17). Only at this point will the church be assured that it will continually reproduce itself from generation to generation.

If our ultimate goal of making disciples is to teach persons to obey all of God's Word, we cannot treat small-group Bible study as an option in our churches. It is a necessity for every believer, regardless of age. We never outgrow our need for consistent small-group Bible study. We have not given sufficient attention to the responsibility for lifelong Christian development. In most churches only about 50 percent of the adults are enrolled in Sunday School, and on any given Sunday no more than 50 percent of those enrolled attend. Is it any wonder we are so ineffective in fulfilling the Great Commission? Most evangelical believers argue that the Bible has all the answers to human problems, but most of us would be hard pressed to tell where the answers may be found.

Our church recently decided on a basic vehicle for ongoing discipleship training. This program consists of six seminars: New Member Orientation, An Introduction to the Bible, The Baptist Faith and Message, Every Christian's Job, Discovering and Using Your Spiritual Gifts, and First Missions and Stewardship. As we are training our members in the basics of church membership and discipleship, we also are preparing them for service in the body of Christ in the church family. When members have completed all six of the seminars of the basic First Baptist discipleship program, they are awarded the First Baptist Church Discipleship Diploma. Through this approach, our adult members are not only trained in the basics of what it means to be a church member, but they also are prepared for service. We believe this will enable us to be more effective in fulfilling the Great Commission in our field of opportunity.

This chapter was not intended to suggest that you follow the program we are adopting but simply to encourage you to think seriously and creatively about your church and the Great Commission. Your denomination, no doubt, has equally effective tools to accomplish the work of the church. Use them! Get involved!

Too much is at stake not to take our task seriously. Let's fold up our game boards and refuse to play church. We are the body of Christ, gifted and empowered to serve. We need not settle for weak, ineffective ministry when God Himself "put all things in subjection under His feet, and gave Him as head over all things to the church, which is His body, the fulness of Him who fills all in all" (Eph. 1:22-23). Let's rise up and reclaim our heritage and fulfill our Great Commission.

Notes

1. Harry Piland, *Growing and Winning Through the Sunday School* (Nashville: Convention Press, 1981), 181.

2. For specific suggestions on creating an evangelistic Sunday School, see Ken Hemphill and R. Wayne Jones *Growing an Evangelistic Sunday School* (Nashville: Broadman Press, 1989).

3. R. T. France, *Matthew,* vol. 1 in *Tyndale New Testament Commentaries* (Grand Rapids: Wm. B. Eerdmans, 1985), 415.

16

What Now?

No doubt every reader will come away from this study with unique impressions and commitments. The Holy Spirit always brings conviction in His own special way to every individual believer. I would like to draw certain implications from this study that have been impressed upon me.

1. First and foremost is the basic thesis of the book: We simply cannot afford to play church. Too much is at stake in our communities for us not to *be the church*. If we believe that God has put everything in subjection under Christ's feet for the church and that God is able to do exceedingly abundantly beyond all we ask, we cannot be satisfied with business as usual. The church must demonstrate the supernatural empowering of sovereign God. While Christ's church universal is made up of all true believers in Christ, the stewardship of our membership in the church universal must be expressed through our personal commitment to the local church. This must become

a priority focus in our lives individually if we're going to impact our world for Christ.

2. Scripture demands that we take seriously the matter of church membership. Born-again believers need to be identified and active in a local church in their local community. Our church membership is not an issue of nostalgia or sentimentality. We do not serve the body of Christ by proudly clinging to token membership in the church "back home." The commitment involved in joining a local church indicates that we have a clear understanding of the mission of the church and that we are wed to that mission. I would also caution moving membership to a particular church for convenience's sake only. You should seek out a church that teaches God's Word, embraces sound doctrine, and has a vision for reaching the community and the world for the Lord Jesus Christ. I, for one, want to expend my time, energies, and money in a fellowship of believers committed to being the church. I frequently hear of families who purchase a home in a particular neighborhood because of the school system. To be honest, as a Christian, my major concern when purchasing a home would be my church membership. More is at stake both for my children and for myself in the choice of the right church than in the choice of the right school. We must be responsible stewards in the matter of our church membership.

3. Our understanding of the church should affect our attendance. We cannot be sporadic or even casual when we understand the vital nature of our mission. We must be present for training, encouragement, and mission. In Hebrews 10:19-25, we find a passage that puts our attendance into proper biblical focus. Verses 19-25 explain the basis of our worship. The wonderful privilege to enter into the holy place with boldness and confidence was purchased by the blood of Christ. In Him we now have a great High Priest. Following this declaration that Jesus is our "great High priest" are three "let us" clauses:

a. "Let us draw near with a sincere heart in full assurance of faith, having our hearts sprinkled clean from an evil conscience and our bodies washed with pure water" (v. 22);

b. "Let us hold fast the confession of our hope without wavering, for He who promised is faithful" (v. 23);

c. "Let us consider how to stimulate one another to love and good deeds" (v. 24).

Notice that our worship, our bold and unwavering confession, and our encouragement to love and good deeds are all placed in the context of assembling together with other believers in verse 25: "Not forsaking our own assembling together, as is the habit of some, but encouraging one another; and all the more, as you see the day drawing near." If we are going to be effective in our Christian life and Christian ministry, we cannot neglect assembling together with other believers. Our regular attendance must become a matter of top priority.

4. Our high calling to be His body must affect our interpersonal relationships in the church. We cannot be the church and continue to play our little political games. The witness of the church in many communities has been severely affected by infighting and squabbling. The relationship between pastor and membership is often a community joke. Too much is at stake in our mission to allow such conditions to persist. We must get on our knees together and seek God's healing touch for His family. We must once again become a people who are of "one mind."

The same could be said for many denominations. The politicizing in denominational ranks has done inestimable damage to the church's mission. We must, for the sake of world evangelization, find our common ground in Christ Jesus.

5. Our understanding of our spiritual gifts and our personal calling must lead us to active service in the life of the church. Too many believers view the church with a passive mind-set. They are casual observers or members, but they are not participants. We are all called to service and gifted for ministry. If your church is to be effective, you must do your part.

6. The mission of the church should call us to bold and sacrificial giving. We are constantly bombarded with the statistic that 20 percent of the people contribute 80 percent of the church's income. If that's true, it is no wonder that most churches remain ineffective. If we truly believe that the work of the church is more critical than any other earthly endeavor, why do we continue to support it with token gifts? It appears to me that our financial support of the church reveals how seriously we take its work. If our understanding of the church is such that it is little more than a community convenience, it will be reflected in our giving.

The other day I was at a luncheon meeting with community

business leaders. The program concerned a proposed community cultural facility. The speaker was attempting to raise personal and business financial support for the project. The price tag was well into the multiple millions. I whispered across the table to a Christian friend: "Boy, that money would build a great church, wouldn't it?" He laughed, but he knew I wasn't joking.

The project being presented that day was a wonderful idea. I hope we're able to get it for our community. It will enrich our community culturally. I plan to take my children to visit. Yet it is not as critical to the life of our community or our country as is the work of the church! If I believe in the importance of the church as a Christian businessman, my giving must reflect that conviction. I wonder how many countless millions of dollars from Christian businessmen have flowed into worthwhile, but noneternal, projects simply because we have not fully understood the critical nature of the church's mission. We can do without a community project, but we can't do without the church committed to the Great Commission. Personally, I want to channel my resources into ministries that will determine where people spend eternity.

There may be readers who are thinking, *My little church couldn't use those large gifts.* What would we do with the money? Think globally! Mission organizations are cutting back on personnel due to the lack of adequate funds. Plenty of projects of sufficient magnitude exist to challenge every believer at every income level. We must allow our giving of the tithe and of gifts beyond the tithe to reflect the nature of the church's mission.

7. Our understanding of the church must affect our lifestyles and witness. We must boldly live and proclaim our faith. Evangelism and social involvement are two sides of the same coin. Neither can be fully embraced without the other. We must be the salt and spread the light. If the gospel of the Lord Jesus Christ is the lost person's *only hope,* we must do everything possible to spread it in our community and throughout the world. No excuses are acceptable for the church not to reach its community with the gospel. We must understand that knowledge of the gospel places us under obligation to lost humankind. We must, as ambassadors, be willing to beg them to be "reconciled to God" through Christ.

The game is over! Let's be the church.